ATLAS
OF
UNTAMED
PLACES

ATLAS OF UNTAMED PLACES

AN EXTRAORDINARY JOURNEY THROUGH OUR WILD WORLD

CHRIS FITCH

Aurum
Press

1 SKELETON COAST
2 FURNACE CREEK
3 LAKE NYOS
4 DOME ARGUS
5 CAVE OF CRYSTALS
6 EISRIESENWELT
7 YELLOWSTONE
8 SUNDARBANS
9 GANGKHAR PUENSUM
10 HANG SON DOONG
11 DARIÉN GAP
12 THE SUDD
13 CHALLENGER DEEP
14 NORTH SENTINEL ISLAND
15 KRUBERA
16 MALIAU BASIN
17 GREEN LINE
18 CHERNOBYL EXCLUSION ZONE
19 THE DEMILITARISED ZONE
20 THE ROCKY MOUNTAIN ARSENAL REFUGE
21 ODESSA CATACOMBS
22 PLEISTOCENE PARK
23 CENTRALIA
24 LAC DE GAFSA
25 MODO ISLAND
26 JABUKA
27 LAKE MARACAIBO
28 QIANTANG RIVER
29 LOUGHAREEMA
30 EMPTY QUARTER
31 THE MOUNT MABU RAINFOREST
32 TREE OF TÉNÉRÉ
33 ININI
34 KAFFEKLUBBEN ISLAND
35 INACCESSIBLE ISLAND
36 DIOMEDE ISLANDS
37 HERSCHEL ISLAND
38 SOCOTRA
39 CAPE FLORAL REGION
40 BIAŁOWIEZA FOREST
41 MERU NATIONAL PARK
42 ENDEAVOUR RIVER
43 TE UREWERA
44 OKAVANGO
45 YASUNÍ NATIONAL PARK

34
37
36
7
20
23
2
5
11
27
45
33

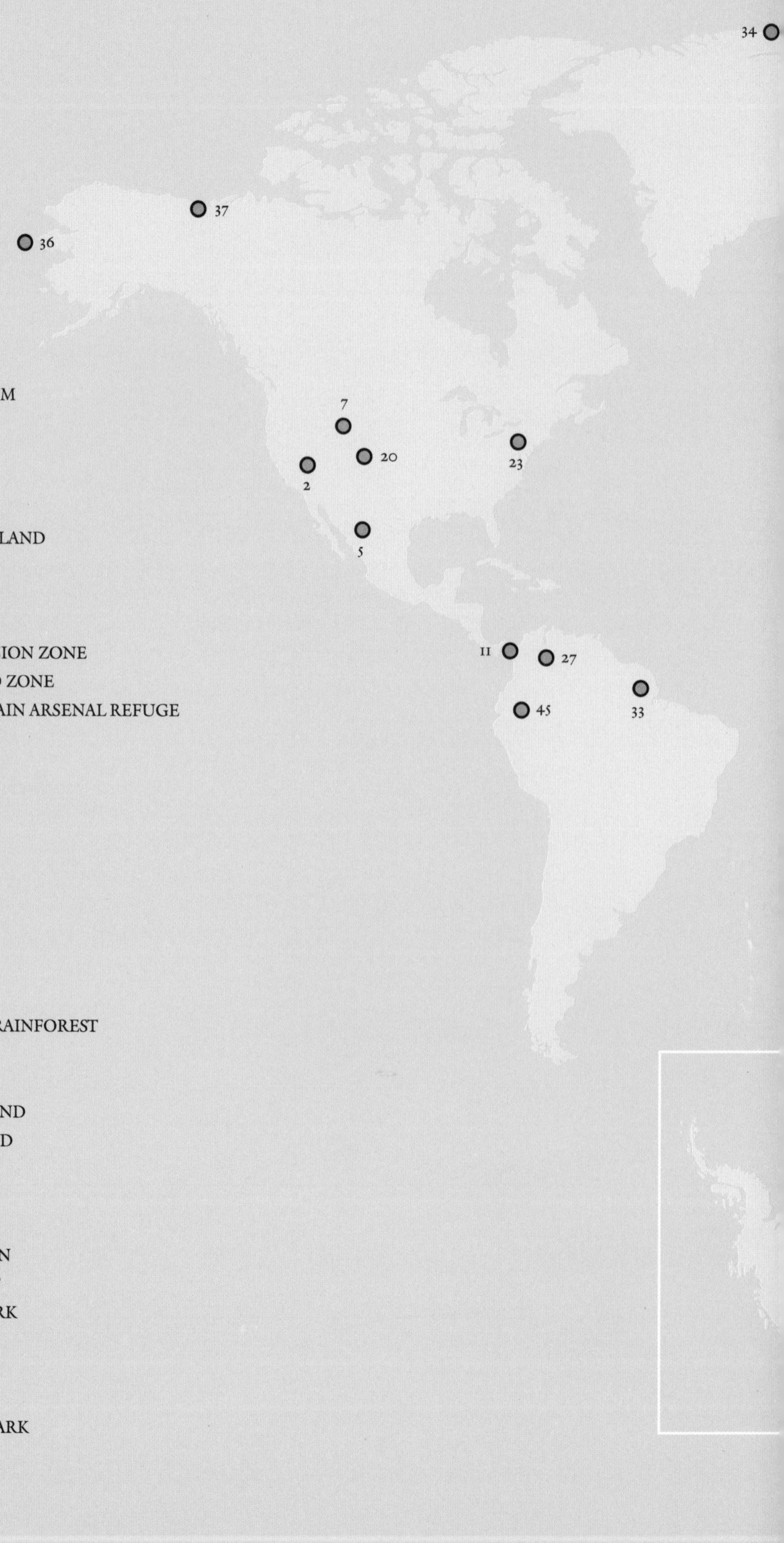

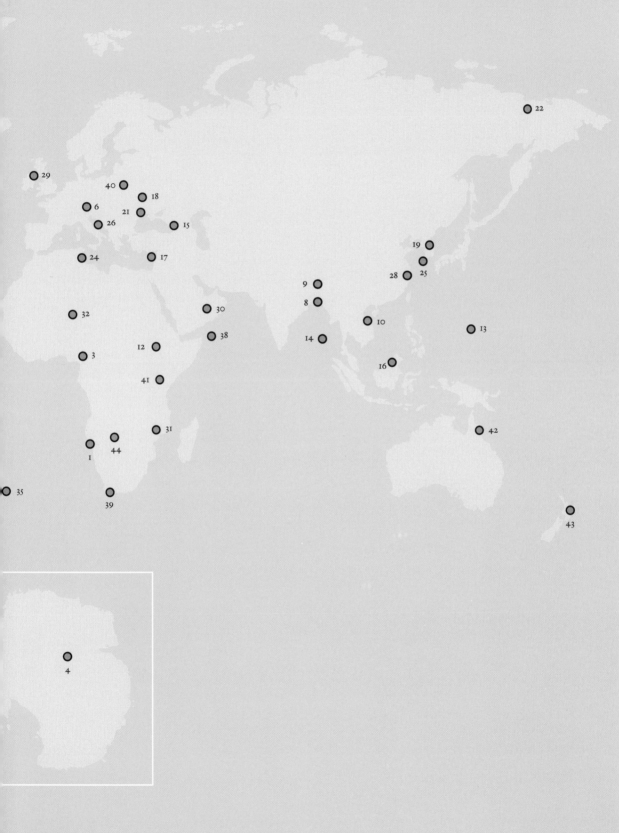

CONTENTS

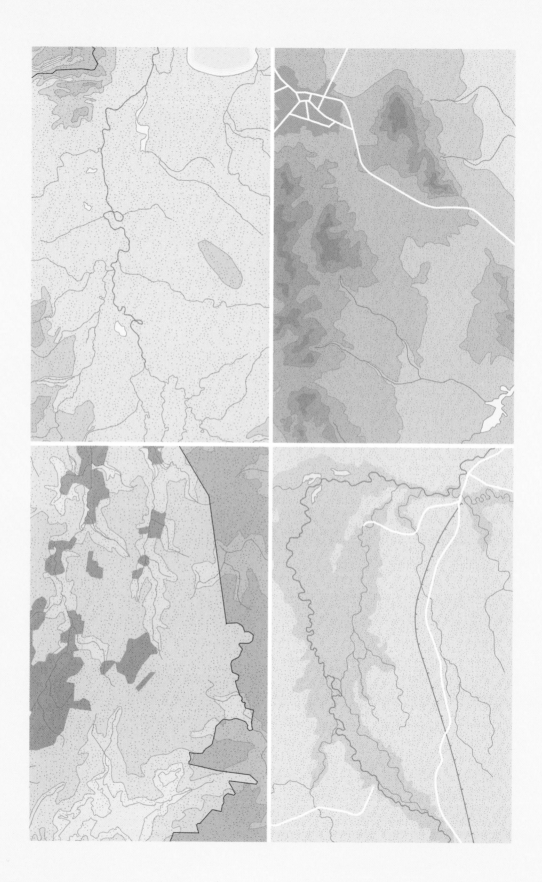

INTRODUCTION

'Wilderness is a necessity,' insisted the naturalist John Muir. Similarly, writer Henry David Thoreau passionately argued that 'we need the tonic of wildness'. While these may be two of the most well-known examples, there has been no shortage of strong words from influential individuals over the years urging us to recognise the necessity of our relationship with the wilderness of the natural world. Equally, there has been just as much written about the contemporary threats facing that same wilderness. While the romantic notion of a paradise subdued by human action may feel like a recent phenomenon, iconic poet William Wordsworth and his contemporaries were angrily arguing back in the early nineteenth century about the apathetic way we were conquering and taming the wilderness that so captivated him.

Two centuries later, it's harder than ever to disagree with Wordsworth's assessment: 'Little we see in Nature that is ours.' Whichever way you look at it, the world has overwhelmingly been developed and controlled. Trees felled, oceans emptied, wild animals eradicated. Leashed and domesticated, the true wildness thoroughly bred out. Previously blank spaces on the map filled in with roads, fields and urban sprawl. The modern era is even on the verge of being officially declared an entirely new geological age: the Anthropocene — the era of man. It's a declaration that confirms humanity as the most dominant force on the planet.

Yet, despite this, aren't we still enamoured by those unpredictable and undeveloped landscapes? Remote and exotic, full of mysteries and unanswered questions – visions of far-flung wilderness tug at our sense of wanderlust. While the so-called 'Age of Discovery', the days of sailing over the horizon in search of new worlds, may largely be behind us (in itself, perhaps no bad thing) it doesn't mean there aren't still many uniquely wild places that we could describe, for one reason or another, as 'untamed'. As 'progress' tames the world, spreading the homogeneous monotony that almost all of us inhabit, these places refuse to comply, firmly resisting the creeping tentacles of development. This book is by no means an exhaustive list of the planet's wildest or most untamed places. Instead, it celebrates forty-five wild and fascinating stories – including isolated realms such as remote islands; unclimbed peaks and other untouched lands; natural wildernesses such as lush forests; extreme environments with intense heat or man-eating tigers; and even towns and other human creations since abandoned, overgrown and reclaimed by the natural world – accompanied by an array of gorgeously detailed maps, which will hopefully inform and inspire.

EXTREME ENVIRONMENTS

ANGOLA

Foz do Cunene

Cunene

The Dunedin Star, 1942

AFRICAN

PLATEAU

N
A
M
I
B

Khumib

Hoarusib

Purros

NAMIBIA

Sesfontein

Hoanib

Kamanjab

Möwe Bay

The Suiderkus, 1977

Terrace Bay

Uniab

Huab

Ugab

Benguela Current

D
E
S
E
R
T

The Montrose, 1973

Toscanini

The Winston, 1961

Omaruru

ATLANTIC

OCEAN

Cape
Cross

The Chamarel, 2012

Hentiesbay

Usakos

The Natal Coast, 1955

Khan

The Zeila, 2008

Swakop

Swakopmund

Vipava, 1968

WALVIS BAY

N

Positions and names of
significant wrecked ships

0   50 miles

0   50 kilometres

Sandwich Bay

Kuiseb

Eduard Bohlen, 1909

SKELETON COAST

NAMIBIA

Namib Desert

'Death would be preferable to banishment to such a country.'

Swedish explorer Charles John Andersson did not mince his words when discussing the possibility of being stranded on Namibia's Skeleton Coast. Many generations of sailors, however, did not have the luxury of choosing between these two options, as instead this inhospitable coastline cruelly inflicted upon them first the latter, and then the former.

The name 'Skeleton Coast', for the northern portion of Namibia's South Atlantic coastline, wasn't popularised until 1944, when John Henry Marsh's book of that name told the amazing story of the ill-fated *Dunedin Star*, a liner whose entire crew had been miraculously rescued after being shipwrecked on the coast two years earlier. It's a rare happy ending for a narrative that has been told time and time again for five centuries, ever since brave and/or foolhardy sailors first attempted the long and treacherous maritime trade route between Europe and Asia which took them around the southern tip of Africa, past what is now South Africa's famous Cape of Good Hope.

Marsh's choice of title was nevertheless apt. First known as a place where the vertebrae and other skeletal remains of many beached whales could be found, in later years the term instead began to refer to the human victims who had failed to find a way out of this wild and unforgiving landscape. The physical conditions off the coast of Namibia make shipwrecks far from an unlikely outcome, as intensely thick sea fog, strong Atlantic gales, and the powerful Benguela Current combine to make it incredibly easy for ships to be driven into shallow waters and onto the shore completely against their will. Aside from the *Dunedin Star*, possibly the most famous of the coast's victims is the *Eduard Bohlen*, a steamer that was grounded in 1909. Thanks to the constant movement of dunes, the coastline itself is in perpetual flux – hence, more than a century since the accident, the rusted hull of what was once the *Eduard Bohlen* now finds itself stranded several hundred yards inland, a striking monument to the Skeleton Coast's vicious nature emerging dramatically from the featureless sandscape.

Being shipwrecked anywhere in the world would undoubtedly be a fairly dangerous and unpleasant experience, but the Skeleton Coast is a different proposition entirely. Assuming sailors survived the rough conditions which led to their beaching in the first place, they would look up and down the coast to find themselves ominously surrounded by some of the hundreds of ships that had suffered the exact same fate. With extreme weather conditions ranging from scorchingly hot during the day and below freezing at night, plus rainfall so desperately low that fresh water is almost impossibly scarce, their chances of survival would be spirit-crushingly slim. Many shipwrecked sailors would lose their minds and begin drinking seawater, a one-way ticket to dehydration and death. Those who attempted to leave the coast and instead seek salvation inland would have quickly made the discovery that there were hundreds of miles of epic sand dunes and lifeless rocky outcrops of the Namib desert between them and civilisation. Many sailors walked incredibly vast distances across the barren landscape before eventually being overcome by the extreme conditions.

Remarkably, there have been people who called this place home. The nomadic Dauna-Daman (which translates as 'seaside people on a desert plain') learned to live with this unforgiving environment by foraging the shoreline, turning any beached whales, seals or fish into food. From the various detritus washed up on the shore, such as whale bones and rocks, they constructed rudimentary shelters to protect themselves from the worst of the coastline's volatile weather.

Modern technologies now enable ships to navigate the misty and mysterious coastal waters of Namibia with far less likelihood of finding themselves stranded on its shores. Nevertheless, the conditions that made it so dangerous continue to this day. Enormous signs plastered in skull-and-crossbones provide an ominous warning to the ambitious wanderlust of passing tourists. Although if the rusty, decrepit corpses of beached ships, doomed to a life of slow decay on the remote coastline, do not provide a sufficiently stern warning, it's reasonable to wonder whether anything could.

RIGHT: The wreck of the *Eduard Bohlen* acts as a reminder of the Skeleton Coast's haunting past.

FURNACE CREEK
USA
Death Valley

'Boys, by God, I believe I have found a gold mine!'

In January 1848, James Marshall struck gold at John Sutter's Mill in the Sacramento Valley, California, and the great gold rush officially began. Despite efforts by Marshall, Sutter and the rest of the men on site to keep their discovery a secret, word rapidly spread around the United States. From across the country, people who fancied their chances of hitting the jackpot packed up their lives and headed west. California's population exploded, San Francisco growing from a population of 1,000 to more than 20,000 in just two years.

The most pioneering of all were the so-called '49ers', those determined individuals who were on their way towards California as early as 1849 (from whom the San Francisco 49ers NFL team take their name). Although few 49ers would have been skilled or experienced in wilderness survival, this was not an expedition for shrinking violets; it required coping with alternating intense heat and extreme cold. To reach their destination, it was necessary for all travellers to navigate a trail that took them through Salt Lake City, then over the Sierra Nevada mountains, and onwards towards the Pacific. Keen to reach the gold mines as early as possible, and not miss out on any of the action, prospectors rushed to get across the Sierra Nevada before winter set in, when deep snow at high altitude would make such a crossing impossible.

The travellers of the San Joaquin (Sand Walking) Company, a wagon trail with their eyes firmly on the golden prize that awaited them at the end of the journey, were not willing to give up quite so easily. Having reached Salt Lake City in October 1849, far too late to be able to attempt to cross the mountains, they instead opted to follow an

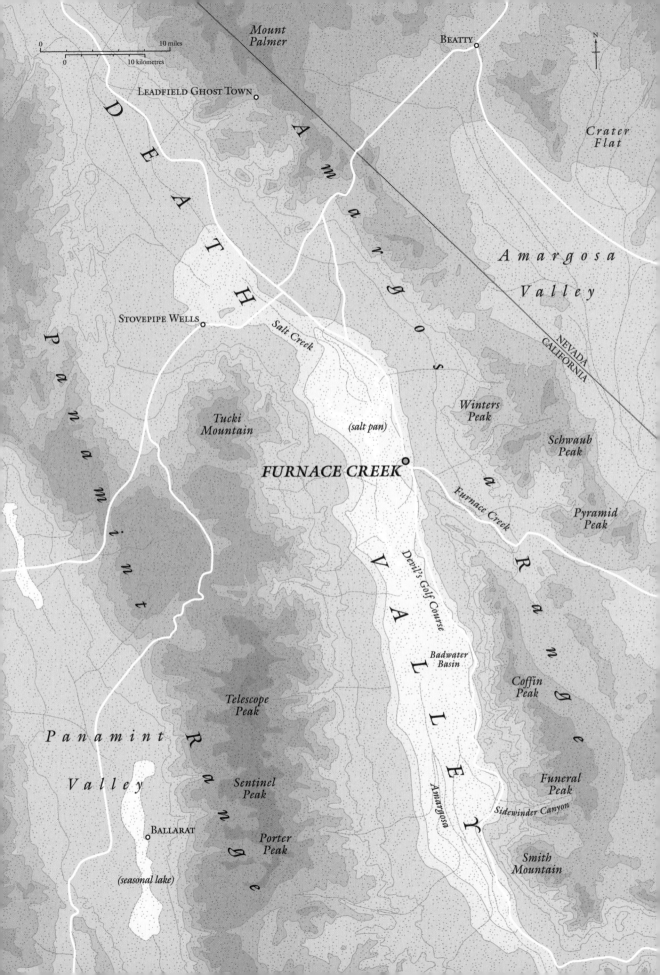

RIGHT: Death Valley's Furnace Creek holds the record for the world's highest ground temperature.

alternative route known only as the Old Spanish Trail. More than 400 people stuffed inside 110 wagons set off together, and successfully managed to avoid the winter delay by going south of the Sierra Nevada mountains. However, they were led astray by rumours of a 500-mile short cut across the desert to the north. A large number of the party, unhappy with their slow progress, made the error of following this new path.

Most people eventually turned back to the original route, but a few stubborn individuals kept steadily marching forward through this desolate, empty desert. Days became weeks. Weeks became months. Fragmenting further as various groups began falling behind, they trudged forwards, tired and thirsty, led only by a crudely drawn map that had been passed around at the point they had left the Old Spanish Trail. Eventually, the lost 49ers arrived at what is now named Furnace Creek. At 190ft below sea level, this is one of the lowest points in the world, and receives less than 2 inches of rain annually. It was not the place they wished to find themselves after a gruelling two months of walking blindly across this barren landscape. Many oxen were weak and incapable of pulling them much further, while the wagons were in poor shape. On both sides, they were penned in by the steep Panamint Mountains and the route ahead offered nothing more promising than a never-ending dry valley all the way to the horizon. Only after two of the younger men in the group completed a 250-mile, month-long trek to Ranch San Francisco and back for supplies were the lost 49ers finally able to leave their hellish experience. 'Goodbye, Death Valley,' someone is supposed to have declared, as the group finally scrambled out of the desert.

The modern but equally inhospitable Death Valley is, at over 5,000 square miles, the second largest national park in the US (behind Alaska's gigantic Wrangell–St Elias, over four times larger). Despite the network of roads and small towns which have cropped up in the valley since the days of the 49ers, 91 per cent of the rugged landscape is still officially designated as wilderness. This includes the deep canyons, arid salt flats and harsh terrain of this part of the scorching Mojave Desert, as well as the 156-mile-long Death Valley itself. It's home to a variety of wild animals, everything from reptiles like the desert tortoise and horned lizard, to predators such as coyote, bobcats and mountain lions, all of which are specially adapted to the extreme conditions.

This intense natural landscape has been traditionally called home by the native Timbisha Shoshone tribe, who have lived here since long before European colonisers arrived. Seasonally migrating across the land, they live off a diet of locally harvested pinyon pine nuts, mesquite beans and other fruit, plants and seeds. The modern community comprises no more than fifty to sixty individuals.

It would have been little comfort to the 49ers to have known that conditions could have been considerably worse for them. A severe lack of water may have been the brutal factor during their harrowing experience, but at least they were trekking through late autumn and early winter. Had they attempted to cross Death Valley during the summer, they would likely have been confronted by the extreme temperatures that have been recorded on the site. The official world record, measured on 10 July 1913, is 56.7°C (134°F), while on 15 July 1972 an immense ground temperature of 94°C (201°F) was taken.

SUBUM
Village

NYOS VILLAGE

CHA
Village

0   1000 yards
0   1000 metres

rim of volcanic crater

L A K E

N Y O S

Increasing toxicity with lake depth

-25   -50   -75   -100   -125   -150   -175   -200   -225   metres

August 1986 Lake Nyos disaster, toxic gas
flow and approximate area of posioning

N

LAKE NYOS

CAMEROON

Nyos

Thursday, 21 August 1986, was a fairly typical day in Nyos, northwest Cameroon. Farmers went to market, children went to school, and people generally went about their daily business. It was, to all intents and purposes, an entirely unremarkable day. However, around 9 p.m., as the heavy rains that had been falling throughout the day finally ceased, the nearby Lake Nyos, shimmering in the moonlight, began to stir. Suddenly, out of nowhere, a great explosion erupted from the surface, jets of water bursting high into the starry night sky.

Unknown to anyone, Lake Nyos held a deadly secret. For many years, a large body of water, dense with dissolved carbon dioxide, had been growing in the depths of the lake from gases released as a by-product of a pocket of magma sitting roughly 50 miles below the lake. This was all thanks to its unique positioning, perched on the edge of a supposedly extinct volcano within Cameroon's Oku Volcanic Field. Originally anchored at the bottom of the lake due to the dense carbon dioxide-rich water being heavier than the surrounding water, over time the pressure had been incrementally building. As this pressure grew and grew, the concentration of carbon dioxide eventually reached a tipping point – possibly due to some unknown trigger event – and collected enough momentum for it to begin racing upwards, erupting out of the surface of the lake, and releasing roughly 1.6 million tons of carbon dioxide into the immediate aerial environment. Unfortunately, such large and dense concentrations of the gas, heavy enough to remain weighed down close to the ground, are not only invisible but also highly toxic to humans and many other living organisms, causing asphyxiation, suffocation and death.

This poisonous cloud raced silently away from the lake, through nearby valleys at speeds of up to 60mph, swallowing up entire villages as it went. Many people, who were fortunate to be higher up the sides of valleys when the gas hit – experiencing weaker concentrations – reported smells similar to rotten eggs or gunpowder. However, the villages of Lower Nyos, Subum, Cha and Fang were completely blanketed by the gas before, eventually, it disappeared into the night air, diffusing away without a trace.

Come morning, survivors described the apocalyptic scene to be like the end of the world. Villages were full of corpses, many people having died in their sleep, while others collapsed simply walking down the street. A staggering 1,746 people were killed by the lethal gas, including more than 90 per cent of the residents of Nyos. With more than 8,300 cattle and other livestock also victims of the disaster, thousands more people lost their entire livelihoods overnight, causing as many as 15,000 individuals to become displaced from the region.

Lake Nyos is one of only three known lakes in the world to be home to such potentially toxic quantities of carbon dioxide, and therefore potentially susceptible to a deadly limnic eruption, as such incidents are now known. The other two are Lake Monoun, 60 miles to the southeast of Lake Nyos, and Lake Kivu, which straddles the border between Rwanda and the Democratic Republic of Congo. Nyos and Monoun are both part of the 620-mile-long Cameroon line, a chain of volcanoes running from Annobon Island in the Atlantic Ocean northwards through São Tomé and Príncipe, all the way up to where it forms a natural boundary along the border between Cameroon and Nigeria. Lake Monoun had even experienced its own eruption only two years earlier. However, with a much smaller number of fatalities, thirty-seven, this had somehow gone almost entirely unnoticed.

The Lake Nyos disaster significantly raised awareness of the fatal potential of such a specifically tragic mix of geology and human habitation, but that is not to say that it will not happen again. The most significant response to the disaster was the installation of a series of degassing pipes, proposed by the French Ministry of Environment the following year, through a project known as Orgues de Nyos (Nyos Organ Pipes). After a decade of experiments, accelerated by evidence suggesting that concentrations of carbon dioxide in Lake Nyos were again rising towards dangerously high levels, a series of pipes were installed in the lake, first in 2001, and extended in 2011. These release pressure from the base of the lake, and – in theory – prevent carbon dioxide from again building up to a level whereby the 1986 disaster could ever reoccur. The roughly 10,000 people still living in the 'firing line' of Lake Nyos, drawn by its rich and fertile soils, will hope and pray it is a success.

ABOVE: The deceptively peaceful Lake Nyos holds
a deadly secret.

80° 22' 0" S / 77° 21' 0" E

DOME ARGUS

ANTARCTICA

East Antarctic Plateau

There's cold, and there's really cold. And then there's Dome Argus cold.

Surviving in the Antarctic requires coping with highly extreme conditions, principally the continent's frequent and perpetual habit of temperatures plunging down to -20°C (-4°F) in summer and as low as -60°C (-76°F) in winter. These were the significant dangers that faced ambitious polar explorers through the so-called 'Age of Exploration' in the late nineteenth and early twentieth centuries. Famous Edwardian Antarctic explorers, such as Captain Robert Scott and the rest of his party on the 1912 Terra Nova Expedition, perished in the severe Antarctic cold, a fate met by many other pioneering individuals both before and since. Even as recently as January 2016, the British expeditionary Henry Worsley, attempting to complete his hero Ernest Shackleton's goal of crossing the continent unaided, suffered dehydration and malnutrition, and had to be airlifted out just 30 miles short of his goal. In hospital in Punta Arenas, Chile, he was diagnosed with bacterial peritonitis, an abdominal infection contracted en route, and tragically died shortly thereafter. Life in the southernmost continent involves battling fatigue, depression, powerfully unpredictable weather, a crevasse-laden landscape, the almost impossible challenge to maintain supplies of food and fuel, and, of course, the debilitating low temperatures.

Dome Argus, high in the centre of the East Antarctic Plateau (an elevation of over 13,000ft) is where Antarctica's extreme temperatures really get ridiculous. On 10 August 2010, a new world's lowest-ever recorded temperature was clocked at the site, an unbelievable -93°C (-136°F), beating the previous record of -89°C (-128°F), set at the Russian Vostok station on 21 July 1983. Unlike the Vostok figure, the new reading

ATLANTIC OCEAN

King Haakon VII Sea

Antarctic Circle

Queen Maud Land

Enderby Land

Weddell Sea

Coats Land

Kemp Land

Dome
Valkyrie

MacRobertson
Land

Ronne
Ice Shelf

Princess Elizabeth
Land

Antarctic Peninsula

Palmer
Land

DOME ARGUS ○ 4000m

Wilhelm II
Land

○ South Pole

○ Vostok station

Ellesworth
Land

3000m

Queen Mary
Land

○ Geomagnetic South Pole

Amundsen
Sea

Marie Byrd
Land

Dome
Charlie

2000m

Ross
Ice Shelf

Wilkes
Land

Adélie Land

Ross Sea

Victoria Land

SOUTHERN

OCEAN

0			500 miles
0			500 kilometres

Approximate average winter temperatures °C

	0	-10	-20	-30	-40	-50

was measured through analysis of several years' worth of thermal radiation sensors by NASA's Landsat 8 satellite (the Vostok reading, taken by Russian scientists, therefore remains the world's official lowest recorded temperature).

'We had a suspicion this Antarctic ridge was likely to be extremely cold, and colder than Vostok because it's higher up the hill,' explained Ted Scambos, lead scientist at the National Snow and Ice Data Center. 'By causing the air to be stationary for extended periods, while continuing to radiate more heat away into space, you get the absolute lowest temperatures we're able to find. We suspected that we would be looking for one magical site that got extremely cold, but what we found was a large strip of Antarctica at high altitude that regularly reached these record low temperatures.'

You do not want to find yourself stranded in such intensely low temperatures. At such extremes, the human body is quite capable of shutting down entirely within minutes of exposure, hence Antarctic researchers are equipped with highly specialised clothing for such environments, layer upon layer of advanced technology used to maintain survival in one of the planet's most inhospitable locations for humanity. 'I've never been in conditions that cold and I hope I never am,' continued Scambos. 'I am told that every breath is painful and you have to be extremely careful not to freeze part of your throat or lungs when inhaling.' Indeed, it is possible that -136°F is the lowest temperature which could ever exist in Antarctica, if not on Earth, due to the physical limits of how the surrounding gases, even at such high altitudes, prevent any further heat from escaping into space than already does.

The surrounding landscape of Dome Argus – one of three major ice domes on the continent, the others being Dome Charlie and Dome Valkyrie (also known as Dome Fuji) – is among the most bleak in the whole Antarctic. Roughly halfway between the South Pole and the head of the Lambert Glacier (at over 250 miles long, the largest glacier in the whole world), it consists of a desolate, barren plain atop more than 1½ miles of ice. This thick layer of ice sits upon the thoroughly buried Gamburtsev Subglacial Mountains, a 750-mile-long range that includes peaks up to 9,000ft high. The East Antarctic Plateau is itself so high it receives barely any precipitation at all – making it technically one of the world's driest places – but at the edges of the plateau, the occasional snow which does fall creates glaciers that flow out in all directions towards the coast. Downslope, descending katabatic winds can rapidly escalate and reach speeds of 200mph. As the surrounding snow is stirred up, this can lead to enormous, powerful blizzards that last for days or even weeks.

It's no wonder Antarctica is the only continent that was never colonised by humans; this wild landscape could scarcely be more alien and unforgiving.

BELOW: Antarctica's intensely cold environment can be overwhelmingly inhospitable for human life.

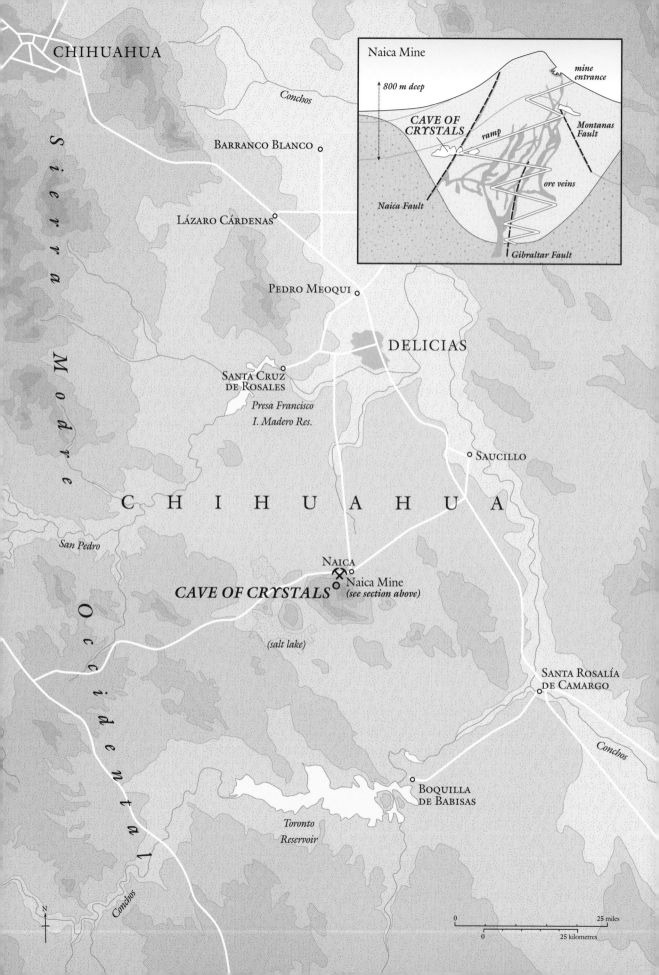

CHIHUAHUA

Conchos

Sierra Madre Occidental

BARRANCO BLANCO

LÁZARO CÁRDENAS

PEDRO MEOQUI

DELICIAS

SANTA CRUZ DE ROSALES

Presa Francisco I. Madero Res.

SAUCILLO

C H I H U A H U A

San Pedro

NAICA
CAVE OF CRYSTALS
Naica Mine
(see section above)

(salt lake)

SANTA ROSALÍA DE CAMARGO

Conchos

BOQUILLA DE BABISAS

Toronto Reservoir

Conchos

N

0   25 miles

0   25 kilometres

Naica Mine

↑ *800 m deep*

mine entrance

CAVE OF CRYSTALS

ramp

Montanas Fault

ore veins

Naica Fault

Gibraltar Fault

CAVE OF CRYSTALS

Mexico

Chihuahua

Francisco Javier Delgado was transfixed. This deep underground, he didn't expect to see anything except the utter blackness of a rocky tunnel, let alone something shining back at him with such intensity. The light was so strong, he felt like a giant eye was staring at him.

It was April 2000, and Francisco Javier and his brother Eloy were undertaking some exploratory mining in the Naica mountains, a region southeast of Chihuahua, northern Mexico, well known for silver, lead and zinc deposits. Indeed, an active mine has been in operation here for over 200 years, with a million tons of rock reportedly extracted annually, equivalent to 170 tons of silver and 50,000 tons of lead.

Instead of locating any of these valuable metals, the Delgado brothers discovered something far more remarkable. Nearly a thousand feet below the surface, with increasingly insufferable heat and humidity, Francisco Javier and Eloy stumbled across an opening in the tunnel rock which gleamed like a diamond whenever light was shone upon it. The hole was small, but Francisco managed to squeeze himself through it, followed by Eloy. In doing so, they became the first people to set foot in what would later become known as Ojo de la Reina, the 'Queen's Eye' cave.

This remarkable space, roughly eight metres in diameter, was filled with giant prismatic crystals, unlike anything ever seen before. Pushing on, the brothers continued exploring, and it wasn't long before they made their major breakthrough, tunnelling their way into a far larger space, horseshoe-shaped and roughly 90ft long, which would later become known as the Cueva de los Cristales (Cave of Crystals). Giant crystal structures stuck indiscriminately out of the floor, ceiling and walls. They were all at least 20ft long – the biggest as much as 36ft long and 2ft wide – making them the largest-known crystals of their kind in the entire world, a record that stands to this day. Not far above their heads, the so-called Cueva de las Espadas (Cave of Swords), with several crystals around 3ft long, had been known to exist for nearly a century. But no one had seen anything on this scale before.

The relentless heat, with the internal cave temperature exceeding 50°C (120°F), and humidity nearly at 100 per cent, made it far too intense for the brothers to stay for more than a few minutes. With the extreme conditions severely testing basic survival in the cauldron of the cave system, further analysis was almost impossible.

It wasn't until the following year that an official exploration could begin, once the various geologists and speleologists who would become the first to scientifically study this historic site were kitted out with the necessary special suits and cooled breathing systems required to spend any significant period of time in the caves. Respectively titled the 'Tolomea suit' and 'Sinusit respirator', these made it possible for humans to spend up to an hour in this otherwise inhospitable environment. Without such equipment, visitors to this extraordinary subterranean world would be sure to suffocate within minutes – a fate that would later befall at least one foolhardy cave-robber.

The consistently extreme temperatures inside the caves are believed to be the reason why the crystals, made of selenite, a translucent, transparent material from the gypsum family of minerals, were able to grow to such a record-breaking size. The accepted theory describes how the limestone bedrock Naica mountains were formed roughly 26 million years ago, on an old fault atop a magma chamber. Over the past half-million years, the caves within the rock filled with the mineral anhydrite, which gradually dissolved as the surrounding rock cooled, and transformed into the selenite crystals we see today. The remarkably stable temperatures within the caves, maintained thanks to the heat emanating from the magma chamber, is what allowed the crystals to grow so extensively. It remains an intense, unforgiving and utterly uncontrollable place, almost beyond the realm of human survival – even with our cutting-edge modern technology.

Humanity's one major impact on the caves is in fact reason to believe the crystals have previously been even bigger. These huge crystal structures grew underwater when the caves were fully submerged by water which has since been pumped out by mining activity. As a result, the crystals have deteriorated in the years since they were first exposed to the air. Their true force has a chance of returning, though: once the current mining activities have concluded, pumping will cease, and the caves will be entirely re-submerged. Then the Ojo de la Reina, the Cueva de los Cristales and the rest of the bizarre subterranean world beneath the Naica mountains will return to the geological wilderness, severing their connection with humanity once again.

ABOVE: Crystals in the Cueva de los Cristales can be
as long as 36ft, and up to 2ft wide.

EISRIESENWELT

AUSTRIA

Werfen

Ascending towards the bolted wooden door, you can already feel the outside warmth being sucked through to the other side. A man wrapped up in thick thermal clothing reaches forwards, unbolts the door, and flings it open. A freezing gale blasts out from deep inside the mountain, extinguishing your handheld gas lantern. With a nod, and a quick relighting, you step forward into the frozen darkness. This is no normal cave; it's a vast network of everlasting ice, the largest ice cave system in the world.

Inside, the floor glistens, the walls sparkling as light from the lanterns illuminates tiny crystals in the mountain cavity. Deeper into the maze, tall natural ice columns, icicles, frozen waterfalls and other remarkable structures grab your attention, as well as enormous otherworldly sculptures, their icy bodies reflecting with a striking azure blue. As the network splinters and fractures into ever-narrower tunnels, climbing deeper and deeper into the mountainside, to a height of around 5,700ft, you eventually come across the enormous Eispalast (ice palace), with ice-lined walls over 23ft thick, and a cavernous ceiling around 330ft high.

Back in 1874, Anton von Posselt-Czorich, an outdoors explorer, was traipsing over the western escarpment of the Salzach Valley's Tennengebirge Massif with a hunting friend when, at just over 5,250ft above sea level, he stumbled upon a funnel-shaped entrance in the west face of the Hochkogel Mountain. He clambered over the scree slope and launched himself into the unknown. Venturing several hundred feet into the earth, he found himself in the most remarkable space: large, silent and full of enormous 'ice sculptures'. Posselt-Czorich had discovered Eisriesenwelt, also known as the 'World of the Ice Giants'.

Although he wrote up a report of his findings in the mountain journal *Jahrbuch des Alpenvereins*, little attention was paid to Posselt-Czorich's discovery for many decades.

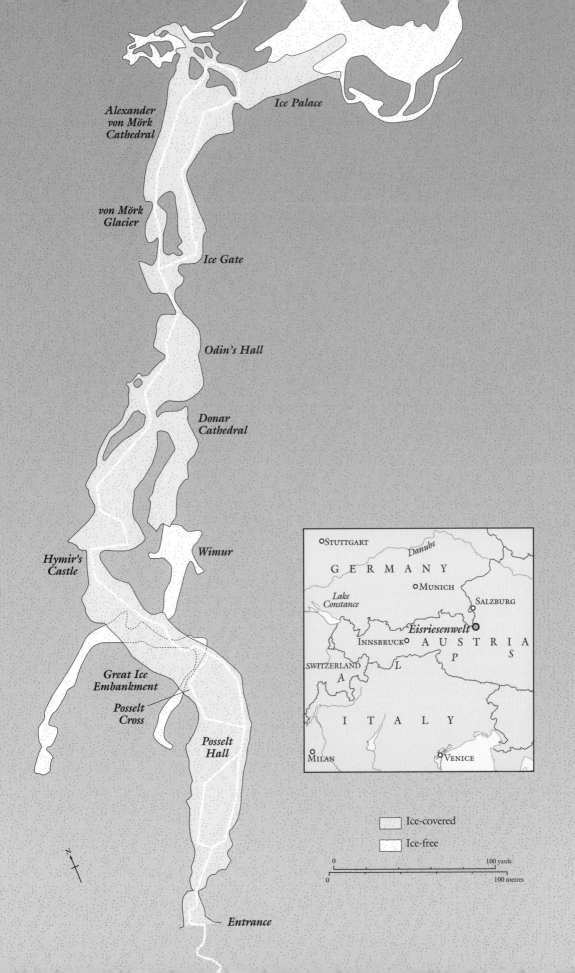

Alexander
von Mörk
Cathedral

Ice Palace

von Mörk
Glacier

Ice Gate

Odin's Hall

Donar
Cathedral

Hymir's
Castle

Wimur

Great Ice
Embankment

Posselt
Cross

Posselt
Hall

N

Entrance

○Stuttgart

Danube

GERMANY

○Munich

SALZBURG○

Lake
Constance

Eisriesenwelt○

INNSBRUCK○   AUSTRIA

SWITZERLAND   L   P
              A   S

ITALY

○Milan   ○VENICE

Ice-covered

Ice-free

0   100 yards

0   100 metres

RIGHT: Eisriesenwelt, the largest ice cave in the world, contains over 3,000ft of ice tunnels.

No one is known to have set foot in the cave again until 1912, when Alexander von Mörk, a young art student and early cave explorer, found Posselt-Czorich's work, and decided to follow up on his initial exploration by delving deeper and deeper into the cave, including past an early ice wall that Posselt-Czorich had been unable to penetrate. Von Mörk returned time and time again to the cave, teaming up with fellow speleologists to explore the vast interior, his findings including the Eispalast and a highly active underground lake, its waves stirred up by the winds hurling around inside the mountain.

Sadly, the First World War interrupted von Mörk's expeditions when he was sent to the front line, never to return. It wasn't until the war ended that some of von Mörk's contemporaries, such as Walter Czernig, and Friedrich and Robert Oedl, returned to keep tunnelling deeper into the cave system. In September 1920, the Eisriesenwelt welcomed its first official tourists, the opening to the ice cave having been developed and prepared for visitors. In 1925, the remains of von Mörk, seen by many as the official true discoverer of the Eisriesenwelt, were interred inside the cavern, as per his wishes.

Modern visitors to the caves, around 150,000 annually, are instructed to wear
thick, warm clothes, since temperatures in the caves can remain stubbornly below zero
year-round. Ice extends for around 3,000ft of tunnels, up to around the Eispalast, after
which the narrow karst cave continues ice-free for an estimated 25 miles, most of which
is yet to be studied to any significant degree. The ice itself is a relatively recent addition
to the Eisriesenwelt; the oldest layer has been dated to roughly one thousand years old,
while the caves themselves were likely formed between 50 and 100 million years ago.
A 2010 study succeeded in scanning the interior of the cave, concluding it covered a
surface area of 300,000 square feet, and enabled the creation of a virtual 'fly-through',
using 262 camera positions to create a 15-minute digital experience. This allows tourists
to explore the underground mountain cavern from the comfort of home, without
the need to try and withstand the dark and cold mountain interior that so captivated
Posselt-Czorich and von Mörk.

44° 27' 38" N / 110° 49' 41" W

YELLOWSTONE
USA
Wyoming

The assembled crowd waits patiently, cameras poised, ready to begin firing as soon as the time is right. The air is hot and thick with the smell of sulphur. Sun-speckled columns of steam waft across the apocalyptic-looking landscape. Nervous eyes begin glancing at watches, feet shuffling uncomfortably. Finally, the spout emerging from the ground in front of us bursts to life, and powerful jets of boiling-hot water begin erupting from the ground, shooting 130ft into the air and leaving only a cloud of mist gently falling away afterwards. For a few minutes, Old Faithful continues firing jet after jet into the air, each one a mini-release of pressure that has been momentarily building deep beneath our feet. With more than 10,000 similar hydrothermal features nearby, such as bubbling acidic mudpots, the Mammoth Hot Springs and other icicle-like limestone travertine terraces, and the vibrant rainbow colours of the world-famous Grand Prismatic Spring, it is clear that something is very unusual about this landscape.

Supervolcano. A word that at first appears to exist purely to appease the makers of Hollywood's disaster genre, is nonetheless a real, physical feature found dotted around a few specific locations on the planet. Supervolcanoes are defined as eruptions that reach magnitude 8 on the Volcano Explosivity Index (VEI), meaning they emit in excess of 1,000 cubic kilometres (240 cubic miles) of ash, lava, pumice and other volcanic materials.

The most famous of all supervolcanoes has to be the Yellowstone Caldera, a 45 x 30-mile basin surrounding Yellowstone National Park, Wyoming (spilling across into Montana and Idaho), which sits atop a 125-mile-deep funnel of molten rock. 'The Yellowstone region is essentially a giant, slumbering volcano that huffs upwards and puffs downward over the decades, like a breathing beast,' writes geologist Robert B. Smith in his book *Windows into the Earth*. The last-known eruption at Yellowstone occurred over 600,000

years ago, yet this cauldron has repeatedly exploded on an unfathomable scale, including 2.1 million years ago, when unimaginably large ash clouds buried half the United States in debris, as far east as Minnesota, Iowa and Missouri, and all the way down to California, Texas and across the Mexican border.

Today, the Yellowstone Caldera keeps itself quiet, restricting itself primarily to small-scale releases of pressure through Old Faithful, Steamboat Geyser (at over 325ft the tallest in the world) and more than 500 other geysers across Yellowstone, as well as occasional earthquakes and other small-scale tectonic activity. An eruption at Yellowstone tomorrow would likely obliterate the National Park, and again blanket vast areas of North America with thick ash deposits. Enormous emissions of volcanic gases such as carbon dioxide and sulphur dioxide into the atmosphere would have dramatic impacts on the global climate, in ways almost impossible to accurately predict. An estimated 87,000 people would be killed overnight. 'Devastation would be complete and incomprehensible at the caldera,' writes Smith. 'Every road, every lodge, every campground, every visitor centre, every geyser and scenic feature would either be blown instantly off the face of the Earth or swallowed as the floor of the caldera sank downward during the eruption.'

Thankfully, such an eruption is likely to give at least a year's notice. Furthermore, with the chances of a supervolcano eruption at Yellowstone estimated at only one in every 730,000 years, it's certainly not a frequent event.

ABOVE: The Grand Prismatic Spring, a central landmark of the Yellowstone Caldera, is the largest hot spring in the USA.

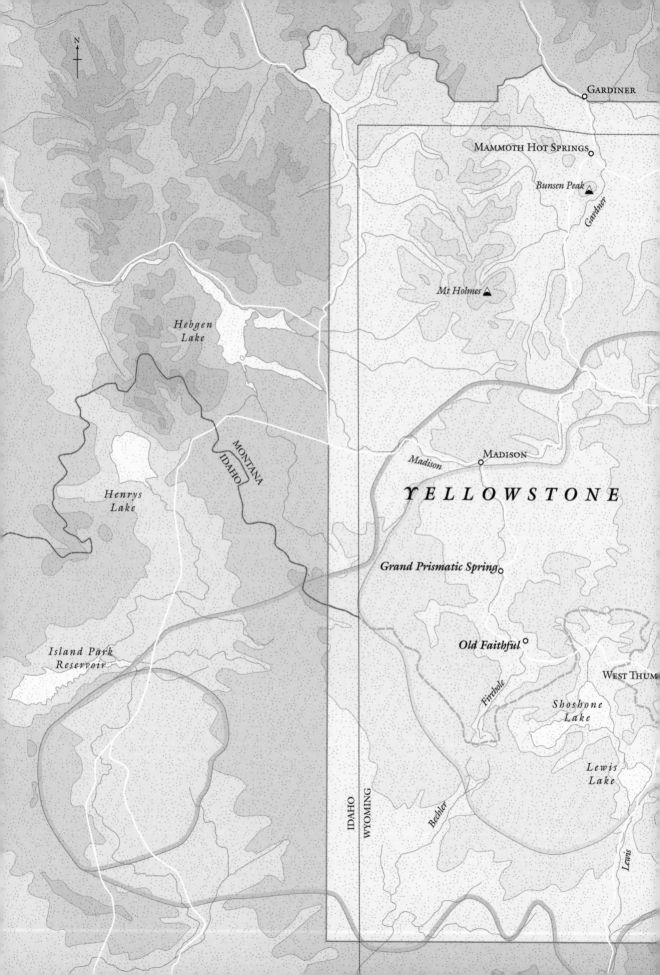

N

GARDINER

MAMMOTH HOT SPRINGS

Bunsen Peak ▲

Gardiner

Mt Holmes ▲

*Hebgen
Lake*

MONTANA
IDAHO

Madison MADISON

Y E L L O W S T O N E

*Henrys
Lake*

Grand Prismatic Spring ○

Old Faithful ○

WEST THUMB

*Island Park
Reservoir*

Firehole

*Shoshone
Lake*

*Lewis
Lake*

IDAHO
WYOMING

Bechler

Lewis

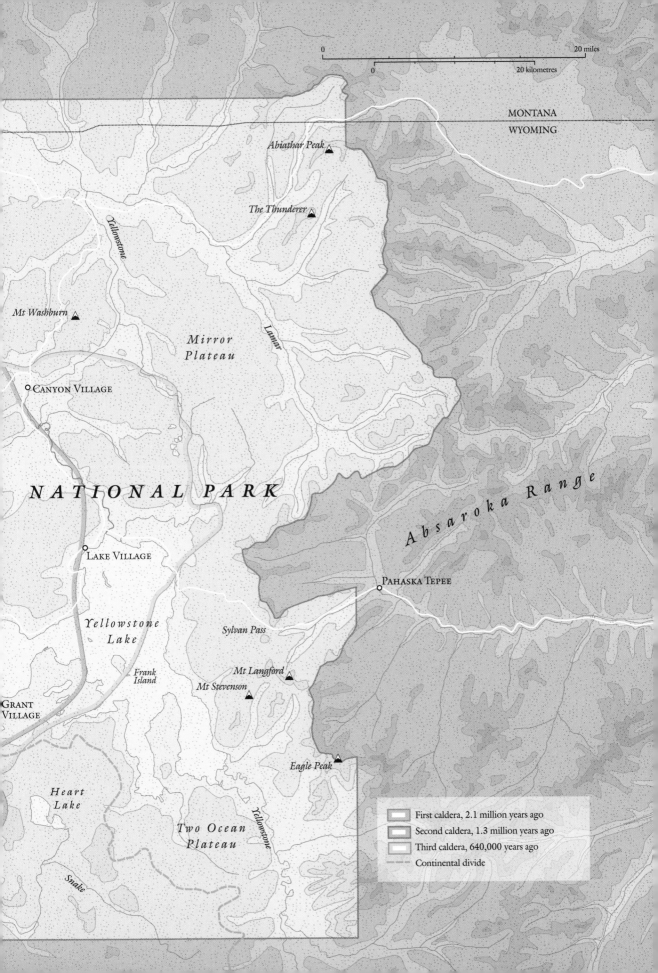

0   20 miles

0   20 kilometres

MONTANA

WYOMING

Abiathar Peak

The Thunderer

Yellowstone

Mt Washburn

Mirror Plateau

Lamar

CANYON VILLAGE

NATIONAL PARK

Absaroka Range

LAKE VILLAGE

Yellowstone Lake

PAHASKA TEPEE

Sylvan Pass

Frank Island

Mt Langford

GRANT VILLAGE

Mt Stevenson

Eagle Peak

Heart Lake

Two Ocean Plateau

Yellowstone

Snake

	First caldera, 2.1 million years ago
	Second caldera, 1.3 million years ago
	Third caldera, 640,000 years ago
---	Continental divide

25 miles

25 kilometres

Hooghly

HOOGHLY

HABRA

BANGAON

JESSORE

NARAIL

Kobotakbho

GOPALGANJ

Rupsha

KHULNA

B A N G L A D E S H

SATKHIRA

Ichhamati

CHALNA

BAGERHAT

KOLKATA

HASNABAD

MONGLA

RAJPUR
SONARPUR

I N D I A

Matla

Bidyadhari

Shibsa

Pashur

Sela

Arpangasia

S U N D A R B A N S

Matla

Raimangal

Malancha

Kanga

Thakuran

Gonshaba

Harinbhanga

*Bulcherry
Island*

Bob Island

N

B A Y   O F   B E N G A L

SUNDARBANS
India/Bangladesh

Ganges Delta

Squeezed on a few small, marshy islands at the end of the gigantic delta that sees the Ganges and Brahmaputra rivers flow through uninhabitable mangrove swamps before emptying into the Bay of Bengal, the residents of villages located in the salty, southern land of the Sundarbans mangrove forest find themselves in a highly unenviable position. The villagers normally eke out a living from harvesting and selling crabs, shrimp and snails, and face a future likely to include rising sea levels gradually drowning their precariously placed homes. It's an incredibly tough existence.

However, there is a lucrative money-making opportunity right on their doorstep. Villagers can brave intermittent, highly dangerous expeditions into the nearby Sundarbans, the largest mangrove forest in the world. Named 'beautiful forest' in Bengali, it stretches for 4,000 square miles across India and Bangladesh. Here, though, they face a toxic mix of potential killers that lurk within. These perilous journeys are made because of one of the Sundarbans' smallest creatures: the bee. Capturing wild Sundarban honey, a sweet and highly sought-after fluid, can mean a significant financial windfall. Despite the dangers, the considerable risks are considered worth it. Although there is a semi-official three-month honey collection 'season', entering the mangroves in search of hives is a highly informal form of employment, so the exact numbers of individuals involved in this activity is unknown. But it is estimated that out of the hundreds of boats that race each other to collect the best honey, anything from 20 to 200 men are killed each year. Their family members back in the village – their wives, parents, children – can do no more than wait, and pray for a safe return.

The dangers they face are plentiful. First and foremost, the hives themselves present quite a formidable foe. Sundarban bees – supposedly some of the largest and most aggressive bees in the world – do not take lightly to having their impressive homes, on which so much energy was expended building them, carved apart so that someone else can benefit from the precious reserves of sweet honey tucked away inside. The poor villagers can afford no protection beyond basic jute masks. Smoking out the bees to try and reduce their aggressiveness, they collectively and calmly carve open each hive as their bodies are assaulted by a great swarm of bees stinging every patch of open skin possible, before rushing back to the boat as quickly as they can.

The bees are, of course, far from the only potentially deadly wildlife lurking in the mangroves. Crocodiles and poisonous snakes stalk the water's edge, while sharp roots and an array of stinging insects make walking on land difficult, and sometimes deadly. Added to this, the locating of hives deep inside the forest means extensive scouting is required before honeycomb harvesting can commence, during which time the villagers are very much at the mercy of creatures far better adapted to this uniquely swampy environment than they are.

There is one species not traditionally renowned for being comfortable in a mangrove swamp which has nevertheless made this particular patch of earth, the marshy creeks and channels of the Sundarbans, entirely its domain. The Royal Bengal tiger is the real threat of this landscape, the creature that strikes fear deepest into the hearts of local villagers. Tiger ambush attacks are the cause of almost all the human deaths in the Sundarbans, and these desperate expeditions in search of honey have unfortunately become a convenient source of food for the tigers. Furthermore, they aren't simply opportunists. Unlike most wild tigers – indeed, almost all big cat species – they appear to have no fear of humans. They are aggressive; hunting not only dogs and livestock, but humans, as prey. Tales abound of tigers actively attacking boats and killing those inside, or even creeping into villages in the dead of night. It is suggested that they developed a taste for human flesh from feasting on human corpses killed by cyclones that occasionally come crashing through this part of the world. Various schemes have been trialled to curb the killings, such as training street dogs to accompany villagers and warn of an imminent attack, but the threat remains high.

Such a dangerous presence requires a secret weapon, and as far as the villagers are concerned, they have one. Before they embark upon their venture into the mangroves, they will gather in a clearing, light incense, put on an exuberant performance of music, and make an offering to the forest spirit Bonbibi, asking her for protection from tigers during their dangerous expedition. Venerated by both Hindus and Muslims in the Sundarbans, Bonbibi emerged at the last minute to save a child when his villainous uncle opted to trade him in exchange for all the honey in the forest. When men are out on a trip in search of honey, she will appear in their dreams and tell them they have collected enough, prompting them to retreat for the safety of the village.

ABOVE: The world's largest mangrove forest is home to plenty of deadly wildlife, including the Royal Bengal Tiger.

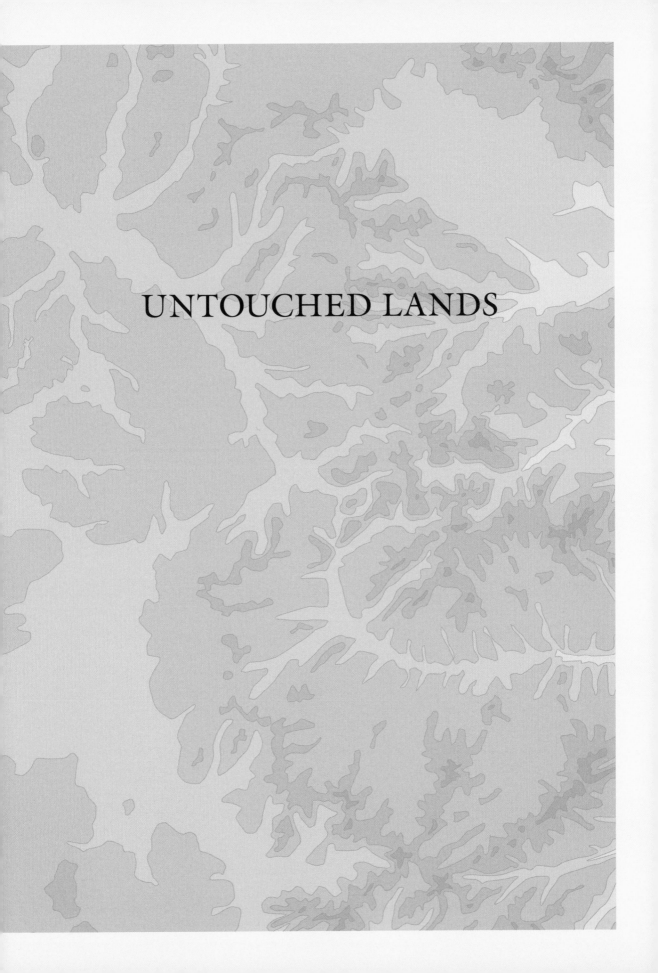

UNTOUCHED LANDS

28° 2' 50" N / 90° 27' 15" E

GANGKHAR PUENSUM

BHUTAN

Himalayas

High in the Himalaya mountains of Bhutan, a heady 22,000ft above sea level, an international mountaineering team had been essentially trapped for five days, waiting for bad weather to clear. Their mission: to be the first to reach the top of Gangkhar Puensum, Bhutan's highest mountain, something they couldn't manage in the current conditions of powerful and unpleasant gales, coupled with almost no visibility. 'Every day the high winds were increasing,' wrote team leader Steve Berry in his report on the expedition to the *Himalayan Journal*. 'The wind was often so strong you had to shout in your partner's ear to be heard. Facing into it made breathing impossible, and the thing was that it didn't gust, it was constant, and it was very cold.' Finally, on 23 October 1986, Steve Monks and Jeff Jackson, two of the team's best climbers, decided to brave an attempt on the summit. Slowly ascending a steep, icy traverse, with strong, freezing-cold winds whipping around them, they progressed just a few hundred feet in four hours, before the impending threat of frostbite forced them to turn back. The following day, Berry made the decision to turn back, and sent the whole team down to base camp, rather than risk losing anyone in the extreme conditions. Their pioneering mission to the summit had been a failure.

Gangkhar Puensum (which means 'White Peak of the Three Spiritual Brothers') may only be the 40th highest mountain in the world, but at an elevation of 24,836ft it remains the world's highest unclimbed peak. It holds this title thanks to the intermittent laws that have prevented people from being able to attempt an ascent, long after similarly elevated mountains across the Himalayas have been conquered. Indeed, a blockade on tourists visiting the country was lifted only in 1974, followed, in 1983, by the Royal Government of Bhutan lifting their ban forbidding anyone from trying to summit five of their highest mountains, including Gangkhar Puensum. Mountaineering has never been a strong

ABOVE: At 24,836ft, Gangkhar Puensum is the world's highest unclimbed mountain peak.

cultural practice in Bhutan, and traditional beliefs dictate that the country's dramatic peaks are the homes of the gods. Suddenly, this ancient country, isolated amid the rugged, unmapped mountainous terrain of the Himalayas, had opened up to the outside world.

With the change in the law, mountaineers were quickly on the scene, competing over who could be the first to sit atop Gangkhar Puensum. Three teams – one Austrian, one Japanese and one American – had tried to reach the peak of Gangkhar Puensum in the year before Berry and his crew turned up, and all had been forced to turn back because of either bad weather, sickness or simply getting lost on the way to the mountain. Berry was keen to succeed where they had failed. His admiration – obsession, almost – for the mountain is obvious. 'I think it is particularly fitting that in a country as special as Bhutan . . . their highest mountain should be no less special,' he wrote. 'Not only is it hard, but it also has that perfect mountain shape with a pyramidical summit, dwarfing all the other peaks around.'

Unfortunately, despite Berry's efforts, the refusal of the mountain's erratic high-altitude climate to clear meant that the climb was a failure. 'We had to put in only the last couple of pieces of the jigsaw for a perfect picture,' he wrote, 'but the whole lot had been blown away by the early winter winds.'

Sadly for Berry, it wasn't to be long before the window of opportunity which had presented itself would close. In 1994, unhappy with the sudden appearance of people scrambling all over their sacred mountains, the government decided to shut off access to all peaks over 6,000m (19,685ft) high, including, of course, Gangkhar Puensum. This was further extended in 2004, to the extent that mountaineering in Bhutan became forbidden altogether. Until the day when this ban is re-lifted, the pristine summit of Gangkhar Puensum will remain untouched by human hands.

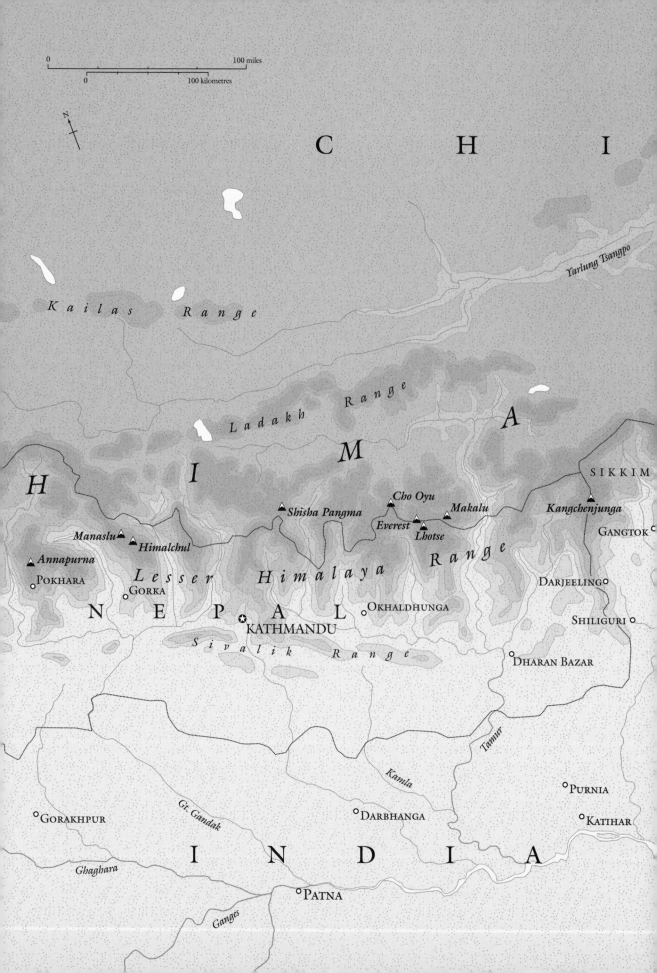

C   H   I

Yarlung Tsangpo

Kailas   *Range*

Ladakh   *Range*

H   I   M   A

SIKKIM

▲ *Shisha Pangma*

▲ *Cho Oyu*

▲ *Makalu*

▲ *Kangchenjunga*

Manaslu ▲

▲ *Everest*

GANGTOK ○

▲ *Himalchul*

▲ *Lhotse*

▲ *Annapurna*

Range

○ POKHARA

Lesser   *Himalaya*

DARJEELING ○

N   E   P   A   L

○ GORKA

SHILIGURI ○

○ *OKHALDHUNGA*

★ KATHMANDU

Sivalik   *Range*

○ DHARAN BAZAR

Tamur

Kamla

○ PURNIA

Gt. Gandak

○ GORAKHPUR

○ DARBHANGA

○ KATIHAR

I   N   D   I   A

Ghaghara

○ PATNA

Ganges

0   100 miles

0   100 kilometres

N

HANG SON DOONG
VIETNAM

Son Trach

It seems impossible that anyone could lose the world's biggest cave. Nevertheless, this is exactly what happened to Ho Khanh, a local Vietnamese farmer. In 1991, he was out searching for rare aloe wood in the Annamite Mountains when gathering clouds suggested a storm was on its way. Desperately searching for shelter from the heavy tropical rain, he stumbled into a hole in the ground. Except this was far more than a simple cave; the feeling of rushing wind and the sound of distant water suggested the presence of a large tunnel, possibly with an underground river at the end of it. Khanh scrambled through the rock and eventually found himself in a huge cavernous space. This region happened to be known for its vast cave networks, but this was certainly the biggest Khanh had ever seen. Having returned home, he tried to retrace his footsteps, but couldn't find it again among the thick jungle of Phong Nha-Ke Bang National Park, near the Laos border. 'I wanted to prove my word, but I couldn't remember the way to the cave,' he recalled to local media VietNamNet. 'It was a wild place, with no human tracks.'

Fifteen years later, Khanh had moved on with his life, having put the experience behind him. But the reported discovery hadn't been forgotten, a team of international explorers wanted to find out whether there was any truth to Khanh's story. Enlisting his help as a guide, they headed into the forest, spending many days over several trips unsuccessfully searching for the opening in which Khanh had once taken shelter. They found several previously unrecorded caves, but none were the enormous one which Khanh remembered.

Then, in 2009, came the breakthrough. 'I stopped by a big boulder,' said Khanh. 'There was the same strong wind, the sound of water running – I knew I'd found the cave at long last. I can't describe my feelings at the time, I was so overjoyed.' The BCRA team,

who had already left the country, immediately flew back in, and followed Khanh for a six-hour trek into the jungle. True to his word, the farmer brought them to an opening that led deep underground. Having navigated their way past a huge calcite barrier they dubbed the 'Great Wall of Vietnam', they entered an enormous cavern – what is now the largest-known cave in the world.

They called it Hang Son Doong, Vietnamese for 'mountain river cave'. Later studies revealed the interior to be over 650ft high, equivalent to two Big Bens stacked on top of each other, and nearly 500ft wide, creating a space through which a full-sized jumbo jet could successfully fly without scraping its wings. The cave interior includes features such as stalagmites that reach more than 250ft upwards from the floor, and the powerful flow of the river which has helped carve these limestone cavities apart for hundreds of thousands of years. So large is the cave, a mini-weather system has been known to occur inside, with clouds forming around the cave ceiling. Contributing to this phenomenon is an underground rainforest, powered by streams of sunlight that squeeze through vast holes in the external walls where the roof has collapsed. This remarkable forest is even somehow packed with wildlife; eagles and hornbills soar through the canopies, while troops of monkeys have made their home in the branches of trees that grow over 150ft tall.

LEFT: The enormous Hang Son Doong was discovered only in 2009, and includes its own underground rainforest.

7° 57' 17" N / 77° 20' 47" W

DARIÉN GAP
Panama/Colombia
Yaviza–Turbo

North, Central and South America are connected by a marvel of infrastructure; the 30,000-mile Pan-American highway. This symbol of prosperity, initially dreamt up as a railway, but later to become the world's longest road, creates a direct link between the wealth and bright lights of the United States of America, and the aspiring economies and societies of Latin America. Two continents are connected by this tribute to capitalism and globalisation, stretching across seventeen countries, from Alaska, USA, down to the Tierra del Fuego archipelago on the southern tip of South America.

However, there is one region through which the Pan-American highway does not run: the Darién Gap. Travellers heading south from the USA can easily cruise along the highway through Mexico, and Central American countries such as Guatemala, Nicaragua and Costa Rica. But upon reaching Yaviza, Panama, 31 miles short of the Colombian border, they can go no further. Their route becomes obstructed by between 60 and 100 miles of thick, impenetrable jungle marshland. To continue, they must head for the coast and get a ship to transport them across the Gulf of Uraba to Turbo, Colombia, from where they can continue into the Andes, and down into South America. Expensive and inconvenient though this process is, it epitomises quite what a formidable opponent highway developers found themselves facing when they were forced to address the Darién Gap. (One unintended but positive consequence has been the inadvertent halting of diseases, such as foot and mouth, which could otherwise have spread across the Gap into Central and North America.)

The Darién Gap, with tropical jungle temperatures over 33°C (90°F) and humidity regularly approaching 100 per cent, is a wild isthmus of exotic plants, large mammals and a smorgasbord of deadly creatures. Hungry Caiman crocodiles and jaguars prowl

this environment, and swarms of malaria-carrying mosquitoes fill the air. A wide variety of potentially lethal snakes can be found across the Gap, including deadly poisonous pit vipers such as the infamous fer-de-lance, a species responsible for over half of all venomous snake bites on humans across Central America.

Outsiders are rarely granted permission to visit, so great are the risks, meaning that vast swathes remain officially unexplored. Perhaps the most famous of all successful crossings of the Darién Gap was part of the first overland journey by vehicle from Alaska to Tierra del Fuego, the British Trans-Americas Expedition in 1972. It required two large Range Rovers and a majority-military crew of sixty-five to get across the 250-mile route they had chosen (the Gap being larger back then, since somewhat diminished by small-scale logging). One member of the expedition was the famous British explorer Robin Hanbury-Tenison, whose personal experiences of jungle life enabled him to spend much of the journey visiting the local Choco and Cuba tribes who inhabited parts of the rainforest. 'While most of the other members were fighting the forest,' he wrote in an article for the *Geographical Magazine*, 'I was lucky enough to be with people who knew how to live in harmony with it. Well over half of the expedition were to be evacuated out with insect bites and upset stomachs during the four months it took to get the vehicles through.'

The illegal drugs trade combined with the Colombian civil war have further made

LEFT: The marshy Darién Gap isthmus remains
a formidable obstacle between Central and
South America.

the Gap a lawless land, inhabited by violent gangs moving cocaine and other narcotics as
well as illegal migrant smugglers. Its geographical positioning as the bottleneck between
Central and South America means that thousands of aspiring American migrants –
primarily Cubans and Haitians, but also Nepalis, Somalis and Pakistanis – dare to enter
its thick jungle land crossing every year, hoping to successfully pass through and onwards
towards their goal. More than 7,000 individuals were recorded attempting to cross the
Gap in 2014, more than double the previous year. Many do not make it out alive. Gang
violence means that the risk of robbery, kidnapping and/or murder is high.

Even without human intervention, attempting a journey through the Gap is
immensely dangerous without the necessary experience and equipment. And for anyone
armed with neither, the threat of getting lost on the dense, rugged terrain or running out
of supplies of food and water far away from civilisation is a genuine prospect.

Nevertheless, the undeveloped nature of the Darién Gap, that which makes it so
hostile to humans, is exactly the same which makes it 'one of the most diverse regions
in all of Central America with an extraordinary range of landscapes', in the words of
UNESCO, the Gap playing host to vast numbers of exotic and unique plant, insect
and bird species. 'The diversity of natural features . . . at the scale of a large and mostly
undisturbed landscape is breathtaking.'

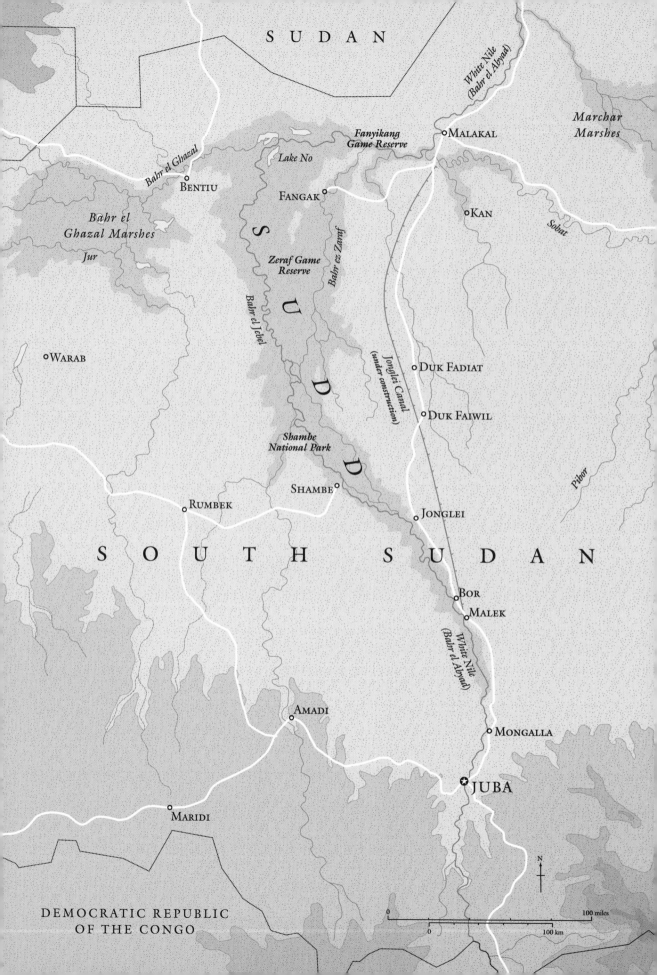

THE SUDD
SOUTH SUDAN

Jonglei Plains

There are few better ways to understand the Sudd's historical role through time than to examine the Arabic root of its name, which translates roughly as 'barrier'. For millennia, people wishing to travel in either direction up or down the Nile, towards the source at Lake Victoria or the mouth where the Nile Delta flows into the Mediterranean, have had to contend with the large, swampy, often impenetrable marshlands of the Sudd wetlands, one of the largest in the world. At Mongalla, as the north-bound White Nile reaches the Jonglei plains, it splits into the Bahr el Jebel and the Bahr al Zaraf and spreads far and wide across an immense area of between 1,000 and 6,500 square miles (expanding up to 15,500 and 35,000 square miles during the wet season) separating into several shallow channels for as far as 370 miles.

In AD 61, the Romans, sent by Nero on an expedition into central Africa, travelled south down the Nile until they were confronted by the immense marshes of the Sudd, where they encountered plants in which they became so entangled that they could cross them only in one-man canoes. Nearly 2,000 years later, the Sudd wetlands remain a large area of utter wilderness. Designated a highly important Ramsar wetlands site in 2006, (so-called after the 1971 Ramsar Convention), the natural landscape, 20 per cent of which consists of three protected areas – Shambe National Park, Zeraf Game Reserve and Fanyikang Game Reserve – is populated by flora such as papyrus, reeds, acacia and water hyacinths. More than 350 plant species have been identified in the Sudd, as well as 100 fish species and 100 types of mammals. Wildlife includes over a million migrating white-eared kob antelope, tiang antelope and Mongalla gazelle, as well as crocodiles, hippopotamuses and thousands of elephants, according to a 2007 Wildlife Conservation Society aerial survey, which concluded it 'could represent the biggest migration of large mammals on Earth'. Shoebill storks and migrating white pelicans, black-crowned cranes and white-winged black terns number among the 470 bird species found on the site.

One key reason why this area – Africa's largest intact area of savannah, as much as three times larger even than Tanzania's Serengeti – has managed largely to avoid human interference, has been the historical political divisions between South Sudan and its neighbouring countries. As far back as 1938, while the region was administered by the joint Anglo-Egyptian Condominium for the first half of the twentieth century, proposals were drawn up to construct a lengthy waterway – the Jonglei Canal – which would stretch hundreds of miles from Jonglei to Malakal, bypassing the Sudd entirely, and significantly easing connectivity between the upper and lower sections of the White Nile. After several decades of delay, the Sudanese and Egyptian governments finally began excavations in 1978. However, plans had to be shelved as geopolitics intervened again in 1984, when warring rebels destroyed much of the essential machinery with the project only two-thirds complete. It wasn't until the end of the war, in 2005, that it became possible to consider resuming construction, yet by this time the Sudd had become caught up in the 2011 Sudanese independence referendum that ultimately saw the country carved in two.

As South Sudan, itself now beset by internal conflict, attempts to establish itself as an independent nation, the revitalisation of the 225-mile canal project has once again been put back on the table. Yet the project has repeatedly raised concerns about the detrimental impact it would be likely to have on the environment. In particular, it is estimated that such a development would potentially lead to a vast emptying of the natural marshlands by as much as 43 per cent, equating to between 700–900 million cubic feet of water being diverted daily, severely interfering with the natural rhythms established over many generations.

The Sudd's waterworld is also home to numerous indigenous Nilotes populations, such as the Dinka and the Nuer pastoralists, who depend heavily on the annual floods to provide the food for grazing as many as 700,000 cattle on the marshy land, and the Shilluk, who take advantage of the vast fish resources presented by the Sudd (overall populations number between 500,000 and 800,000, according to surveys taken in the 1980s). Their unique lifestyles – which managed to survive over two decades of civil war – is under threat. The true strength of the Sudd 'barrier' looks likely to be tested in the coming years.

RIGHT: Antelope and gazelle thrive among the wetlands of the Sudd.

CHALLENGER DEEP

USA

Mariana Trench, Guam

'I'm not sure yet if there really is a solid surface. The water is gin-clear. I can see far into the distance: nothing. The bottom is utterly uniform, devoid of any character but the absence of character, of dimension and direction. I've seen seafloors in more than 80 deep-ocean dives. Nothing like this. Nothing.'

When James Cameron reached the ocean seabed in the submarine *Deepsea Challenger* on 26 March 2012, as described above for *National Geographic*, he achieved something accomplished by only two other people in all of human history. Cameron – who counts blockbusters *Titanic*, *Avatar*, *Aliens* and *The Terminator* among his directorial portfolio – had just become the first person to undertake a solo mission to Challenger Deep, the deepest-known part of our planet's oceans. An incredible 35,787ft below the surface of the waves, this remote spot in the Pacific Ocean's Mariana Trench, on the southern end of the arch of the Mariana Islands, is more than a mile deeper than Mount Everest is tall, deeper even than the regular cruising altitude of commercial aircraft.

With close to freezing temperatures, permanent darkness and miles of ocean squashing down from above – eight tons per square inch, one thousand times stronger than normal atmospheric pressure – it's an intense environment in which to live. Marine biologists and oceanographers had no idea whether life could even survive at such depths. Until 1960, that is, when marine biologist, engineer and explorer Jacques Piccard, together with his assistant, US Navy Lieutenant Don Walsh, became the first people to make the epic and iconic journey to the bottom of the sea in the tiny US Navy submarine *Trieste* (a blimp-like 'bathyscaphe'). Because of the strong and thick walls required to prevent their vessel being crushed by the immense water pressure,

Rota

Guam

P A C I F I C

O C E A N

T
R
E
N
C
H

M
A
R
I
A
N
A

CHALLENGER DEEP ○

Ocean depths (metres)

-10,000   -8,000   -6,000   -4,000   -2,000

N

0   50 miles

0   50 km

the pair squashed inside an incredibly cramped interior, only 76 inches in diameter. Piccard recorded he was unable to fully stretch his arms when inside.

With a sense of trepidation, Piccard and Walsh gradually descended into the unknown, waiting patiently for hour upon hour to see what mysteries they might find in this, the deepest, darkest pocket of the ocean. The historic seven-mile journey directly downwards lasted an incredible five hours. Silently staring out of their porthole at the vast ocean, upon which no human had ever gazed before, their vessel finally came to a halt. History was made at 13:06, 23 January 1960, as they arrived at the very bottom of the seabed, gently bumping along 'a carpet of uniform ivory color' as Piccard described it, also for *National Geographic*. Silt was stirred up by their arrival, preventing them from taking any photographs of the barren marine landscape.

Due to the brief window of daylight they were afforded before they needed to be back at the surface, they had a mere twenty minutes at the bottom before they had to begin the return journey. Squinting through the gusts of silt spiralling all around them, they spotted an alien creature illuminated by the headlights of the *Trieste*. Appearing uncomfortable in the lights, the creature squirmed away into 'the eternal night which was its domain'. It was around a foot-and-a-half long, Piccard identifying it as a kind of flatfish. After centuries of wondering and theorising, here was definitive evidence that even at the deepest point in the ocean, life could find a way to survive.

Over half a century later, Cameron's expedition was to be the first manned journey to Challenger Deep since Piccard and Walsh. On a rough, stormy morning, Cameron squeezed himself 'like a walnut in its shell' into his state-of-the-art sub, the *Deepsea*

Challenger, and braced himself for a long descent into the inky depths. With a vessel fully equipped with a sediment sampler, a robotic claw, gauges for measuring temperature, salinity and pressure, and multiple 3D cameras, a proper survey of whatever can be found at these extreme depths could be undertaken.

'As you start descending, the sub goes very fast. I'm screaming down, and in just a few minutes I'm in water that's 36 degrees Fahrenheit [2.20°C],' he recalled for *National Geographic*, a partner in the expedition. 'All of [a] sudden my feet are freezing, the back of my head is freezing, but the middle part of my body is still warm . . . you're in total darkness for most of this dive, so the sub gets very cold.' After two and a half hours, the *Deepsea Challenger* finally stopped descending. Cameron was able to peer out into the absolute lowest point of our oceans and marvel at the desolate landscape on which he had landed, 'like new-fallen snow on an endless parking lot'.

Unfortunately, with his hydraulic arm eventually failing, and fluid squirting out and blocking his window, his stay on the seabed was limited to only three hours, half the intended time. Despite hopes of seeing an array of deep-ocean-adapted life, Cameron observed almost no signs of life whatsoever, only a few amphipods, very small 'bottom-feeders'. This was 'beyond the limits of life itself', as he described it. 'The impression to me was it's very lunar, very isolated. I felt as if, in the space of one day, I'd gone to another planet and come back.'

BELOW: The US submarine *Trieste* carried the very first explorers to the bottom of the ocean in 1960.

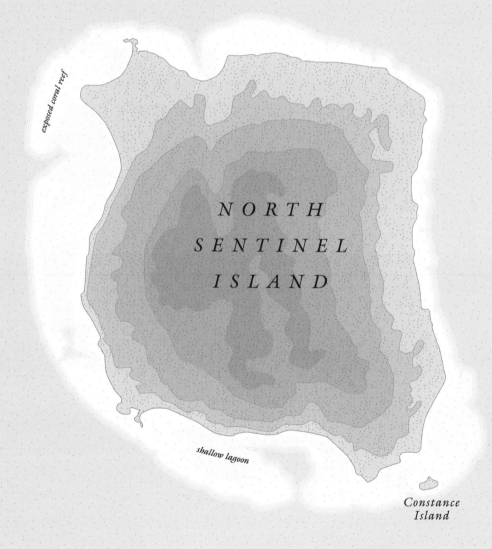

INDIAN OCEAN

exposed coral reef

NORTH
SENTINEL
ISLAND

shallow lagoon

Constance
Island

N

| 0 | | | 4000 yards |
| 0 | | | 4000 metres |

NORTH SENTINEL ISLAND

INDIA

Andaman Islands

It's hard to believe that 'uncontacted' people could still exist in the twenty-first century, in a world bursting with GPS, virtual reality and video messaging. Yet, while they may be few and far between, there are a handful of communities who have successfully defended themselves from intrusions by outsiders, holding on to their unique lifestyles and firmly rejecting everything the modern world has to offer.

One of the most well known – and probably most disconnected – of these communities are the hunter-gatherer residents of North Sentinel Island, a 28 square miles landmass to the west of the main 576-strong archipelago of the Andaman Islands, between the Andaman Sea and the Bay of Bengal. Historically, Andaman Islanders (the Andamanese) have gathered a reputation for aggression towards outsiders; thirteenth-century traveller Marco Polo described them as 'a most brutish and savage race'. However, most of the Andamanese have now been connected to the modern world for several centuries. The British strategically colonised the islands in the late 1700s, and these were occupied by the Japanese during the Second World War. Even the Jarawa of Great Andaman Island, who resisted contact until the late 1990s, eventually began integrating with the outside world following the construction of a main road, many even now learning Hindi instead of their indigenous language.

However, the people of North Sentinel Island, commonly referred to as the Sentinelese, have maintained their opposition even into the twenty-first century. It is believed that they have occupied their island for the past 60,000 years, although the British East India Company's observations of faint lights in 1771 appears to be the first known record of its existence. Experts who have studied what we do know of the Sentinelese language report it to be significantly different to that of the surrounding

islands (even from the language of the Jarawa, from whom the Sentinelese are believed to have originated), suggesting there has been little to no mixing among them and other island communities.

Otherwise, they are a community of which very little is known, thanks to the aggressive response they have adopted towards any outsiders. For example, in 1974, *National Geographic* sent a film crew to the island, in the hope of making peaceful contact with the islanders. Instead, they were assaulted by a volley of arrows, driving the team away, and wounding the film director in the thigh.

In 1991, an expedition team arrived bearing an armful of coconuts as a peace offering, and successfully convinced the man who greeted them by pointedly aiming his bow and arrow at the approaching boat to put down his weapon and accept the gifts. It was the closest the outside world had ever come to making official contact with the Sentinelese, and yet it remains the last significant such occasion, the islanders returning to their hostile stance ever since.

Therefore, analysis of the state of the island has been achieved only from a distance. Aerial imagery shows thick forestry, indicating a community that is quite at home in a jungle environment, but also one which knows how to remain hidden. India's ten-year

LEFT: New coral reefs were exposed when the 2004 Indian Ocean tsunami lifted North Sentinel Island up out of the sea.

national censuses have had to make informed guesses on the island's population based on head counts on the beaches; they recorded 23 individuals in 1991, 39 in 2001, and only 15 in 2011, figures which might or might not give accurate readings for the island's population; nobody knows. The true size of the community could potentially be several hundred.

One major impact to the island which is known about is the tragedy of the 2004 Boxing Day 9.1 magnitude earthquake. This infamously struck off northwest Thailand and sent a powerful surge across the Indian Ocean, causing fatal tsunamis across many countries around the ocean's rim, including Thailand, Indonesia, India, Sri Lanka and Malaysia, and even as far away as Somalia, with more than 225,000 people killed in total. The Andaman Islands lay right in the path of the destructive wave, a mere 530 miles from the epicentre. The entire North Sentinel Island experienced a dramatic uplift out of the sea, with NASA satellite imagery revealing a ring of exposed coral reefs newly protruding out of the sea surface, a significant geological shift that has generally remained in place to this day. The Indian Air Force sent a helicopter to fly over the island in the wake of the tsunami, to which a single Sentinelese man responded by marching out of the jungle and confidently firing arrows in its direction. Irrespective of the major natural disaster that had just occurred, the outside world was still not welcome on North Sentinel Island.

43° 19' 0" N / 40° 37' 4" E

KRUBERA

GEORGIA

Abkhazia

In August 2012, speleologist Gennady Samokhin surfaced from a historic dive, emerging from a narrow underwater tunnel in the world's deepest cave. Five years earlier, the fearless Ukrainian explorer had set a new world record for extending the known depth of this cave, Krubera, by reaching a scarcely believable depth of 7,188ft – the equivalent of nearly five Empire State Buildings on top of each other. But Samokhin wasn't satisfied. Half a decade later, he kitted up again, and headed back into the subterranean world. By the time he returned to the surface, he had broken his own record, confirming Krubera as the world's deepest-known cave system, now known to reach at least 7,208ft.

The Krubera cave system – one of several hundred known caves located within the Arabika Massif region, bordered by both the Black Sea and the Greater Caucasus mountains – was discovered in the 1960s, and named after the famous Russian geologist Alexander Kruber. The wider region of Abkhazia has been a disputed area geopolitically since 1992, when the region declared independence following the collapse of the Soviet Union. The newly independent state of Georgia also laid claim to the area, and officially the region remains a northern region of Georgia. In January 2001, Krubera was confirmed as the world's deepest-known cave, when a depth of 5,610ft was reported back to the surface. With the Ukrainian Speleological Association adopting the target of pushing ever further into the depths of the tunnel network, nine cavers spent seventeen days in October 2004 hauling themselves deeper and deeper into the abyss. Thanks to their efforts, Krubera was assigned a new depth of 2,080 m (6,824ft), making it the first (and still the only) known cave to extend beyond 2km (over 6,500 feet) deep. Thanks to the well-publicised efforts of Samokhin, we know it carries on deeper still – potentially far further.

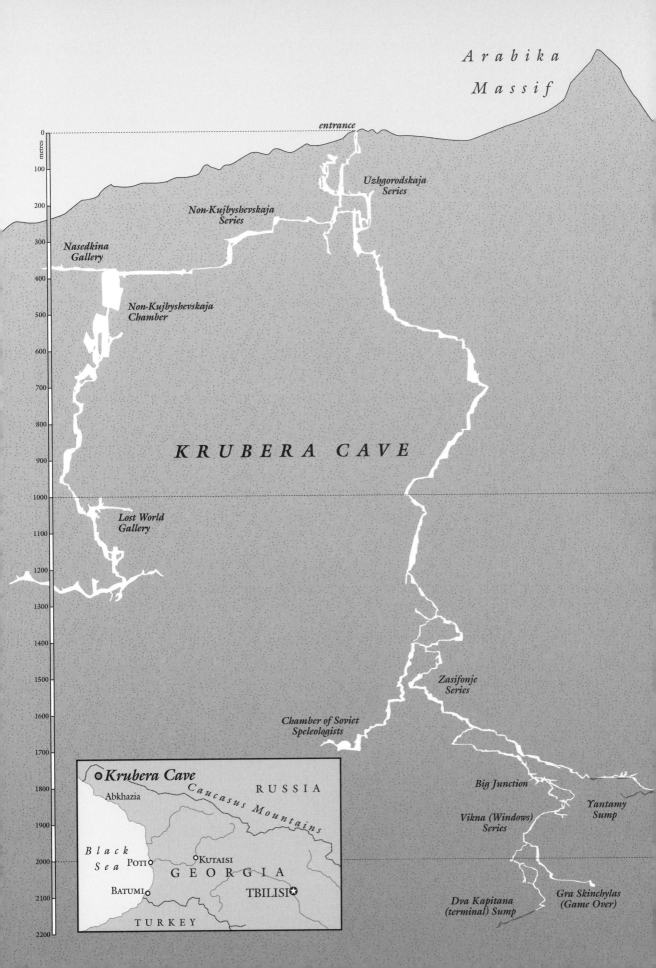

Arabika Massif

metres

0 — entrance

100

200 — Uzhgorodskaja
Series

300 — Non-Kujbyshevskaja
Series

Nasedkina
Gallery

400

500 — Non-Kujbyshevskaja
Chamber

600

700

800

KRUBERA CAVE

900

1000

Lost World
Gallery

1100

1200

1300

1400

Zasifonje
Series

1500

1600 — Chamber of Soviet
Speleologists

1700

1800 — Big Junction

Vikna (Windows)
Series

Yantamy
Sump

1900

2000

Dva Kapitana
(terminal) Sump

Gra Skinchylas
(Game Over)

2100

2200

○ **Krubera Cave**

Abkhazia

RUSSIA

Caucasus Mountains

*Black
Sea*

Kutaisi

Poti

GEORGIA

TBILISI ✪

Batumi

TURKEY

'Like climbing an inverted Everest' is how one team member of a *National Geographic*-supported expedition to Krubera described the experience. Such depth involves plenty of practices that mountaineers might well recognise, including the creation of 'camps' en route, at strategic places below the surface. At these camps, exhausted cavers are able to cook food, then scramble into their tents and huddle together for warmth while they sleep – temperatures in the cave typically increase with depth, but they can still drop to as low as 2°C (36°F) – before they then wake and commence another twenty-hour day. Studying a detailed cross-sectional map of the tunnels allows the rest of us mere mortals to envisage undertaking such an epic journey deep beneath the Earth's surface. It's a terrifying imagination game, a claustrophobic nightmare descent into the depths of this cold, dark, wet mountain interior.

The cave entrance itself sits at a significant 7,350ft above sea level. Initially, entering Krubera involves fighting past a series of crow nests in the early part of the shaft (hence the Russian name for the cave, Voronya, which translates as 'crow's cave'). This early section held back ambitious speleologists until the 1980s, thanks to a series of extremely narrow twists and turns less than 330ft down. Having successfully cleared this obstruction, and ignoring a number of deceptive meandering routes that shoot off from the main spine of the cave, the route rapidly plunges through the Jurassic-era limestone rock. Water trickles all the way down through these tight channels on the descent, its natural route from the top of the mountain to the level of the water table thousands of feet below, especially during summer when snow settled at high altitude finally melts away. This process naturally enables various specialist, peculiar-looking life forms – everything from beetles to millipedes, spiders to shrimp – to make their home in this most lonely and unusual of habitats. At 4,600ft down, a series of narrow submerged tunnels (known as siphons, or sumps) need to be negotiated, which requires the adoption of highly skilled cave-diving techniques. Continuing the descent through the earth, a similar situation awaits cave explorers at 7,000ft down, where the tunnel disappears into the deepest-known sump.

This terrifyingly dark and isolated location is known casually as the 'terminal siphon', from where it would be essentially impossible to get any external help if anything went wrong. Here Samokhin has – twice – made his record-making dives, and presumably will one day be keen to do so again. Of course, it may be far from the bottom; Samokhin has commented that he believes it could even be as long as 33,000ft, all the way to the Black Sea. No surprise, therefore, that Krubera is informally known as being the world's 'bottomless' cave.

LEFT: Exploring the depths of Krubera has been compared to 'climbing an inverted Everest'.

MALIAU BASIN

MALAYSIA

Sabah, Borneo

In 1947, the pilot of a light aircraft found himself lost while flying over the thick, dense, and seemingly impenetrable rainforest of Sabah, northern Borneo. Tracking back and forth across the never-ending forest below, thick with greenery and shrouded in mist, he suddenly found himself facing a sheer cliff that had emerged from the clouds. Taking evasive action to prevent a horrific crash, he realised he had become penned in by steep, incredibly tall slopes on all sides. Amazingly, he had accidentally stumbled upon an enormous, unmapped basin, as far as 15 miles across, of which the outside world had absolutely no knowledge.

The local indigenous Tenggara Murut (hill people) and Orang Sungai (river people), however, had always known of this remarkable location, and their name for it, 'Maliau', which translates roughly as either 'bowl' or 'basin', forms our name for it today: the Maliau Basin. Nevertheless, they did not venture into the bowl that they referred to as the 'mountain of stairs' (in reference to the many waterfalls pouring from the steep cliffs around the edge). Much of their hesitation stemmed – understandably – from the belief that a fierce dragon lives in what is now known as Lake Linumunsut, located at the base of the sheer cliff face of the basin's northern rim. Local legends claim the dragon holds back the lake's water with its enormous tail. It would be several decades before any explorers, researchers or scientists would successfully breach the gigantic natural limestone barriers constructed around the basin (reaching as high as 5,500ft above sea level) which had kept this immense area a treasure to itself.

The first official recorded attempt was in 1976, when a team attempted to cross over the northern rim via Lake Linumunsut. They almost managed to reach the upper escarpment, yet were forced to turn around just forty feet from the top. Follow-up

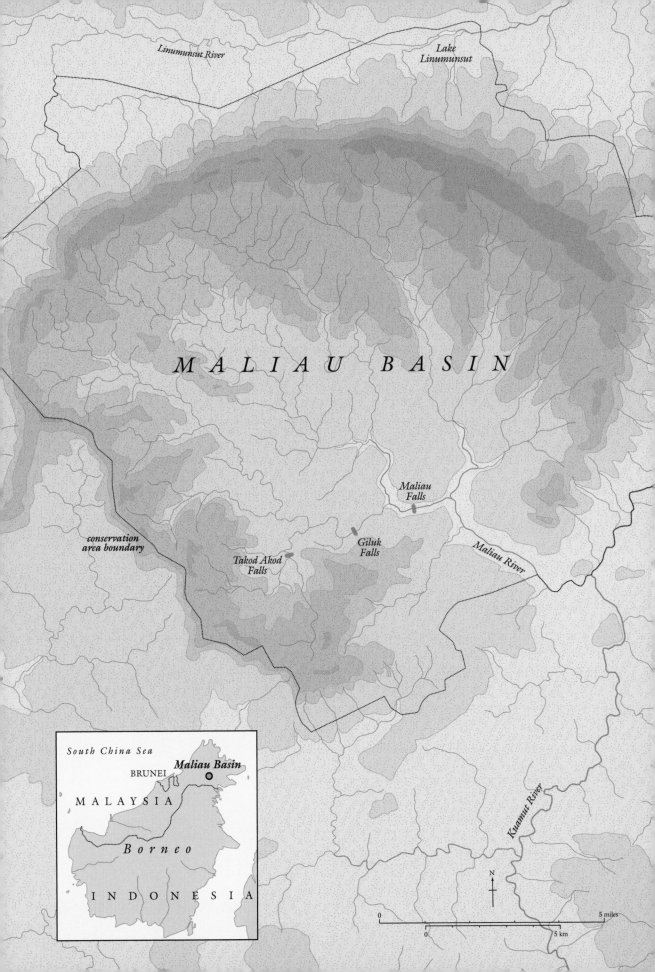

Linumunsut River

Lake
Linumunsut

MALIAU BASIN

Maliau
Falls

Giluk
Falls

conservation
area boundary

Takod Akod
Falls

Maliau River

Kuamut River

South China Sea

BRUNEI

Maliau Basin

MALAYSIA

Borneo

INDONESIA

N

0   5 miles

0   5 km

expeditions were soon under way, firstly by the Forestry Department in 1978, also unsuccessful, and then by a Sabah Museum team that tried to enter via the western rim in 1980. Decimated by bouts of malaria and a lack of supplies, they too had to give up short of their goal. The task was looking increasingly impossible. However, the breakthrough finally came in 1982, when the Malaysian government sponsored a joint military and scientific expedition to travel into the basin by helicopter. Humans had finally penetrated the basin for the first time in recorded history.

The Maliau Basin is home to a vast array of wild species – everything from the critically endangered Sumatran rhinoceros, hunted close to extinction because of the medicinal properties attributed to its horn, to the vulnerable tree-climbing Sunda clouded leopard, a close relative of the extinct sabre-toothed tiger, to the Malayan sun bear (or honey bear, due to their affection for honey), clearly recognisable from the yellow patches on their chests. The surrounding forest also hosts a population of endangered pygmy elephants, baby-faced animals that are smaller but have larger ears and tails than their cousins across the rest of Asia. Furthermore, the remarkable plant life that has been found in the basin has earmarked it as a biodiversity hotspot, even when compared to the rest of Borneo. The basin's unique shape sees the vegetation change rapidly as you scale the cliff; carnivorous pitcher plants and exceedingly rare Rafflesia (often called the 'corpse flower', due to its vile, rotting smell), as well as other species specially adapted to nutrient-poor soils, are found gazing down from above at the lush forest canopy below.

In response to this remarkable biodiversity, the Maliau Basin Conservation Area was made official in 1984, even though it wasn't until 1988 that the first proper scientific expedition to the Maliau Basin took place. Since the scientific community first learned how to access the basin however, it has been a prime location to conduct studies on the relatively undisturbed, almost pristine, environment. The Maliau Basin has hence been the site of many significant discoveries, including the finding of a 294ft-tall Yellow Meranti (just shy of the height of London's Big Ben) by University of Cambridge researchers in 2016, making it – at the time – the tallest-known tree in the tropics. Of course, in such an unexplored region of the world it is hard to accurately measure such giant trees, even with the latest, most sophisticated, state-of-the-art 3D scanning equipment. The only way to know for certain was by employing the services of Unding Jami, an expert tree-climber from Sabah. With a tape measure somehow stored on his person, he shimmied his way to the top of the tree, and confirmed the suspected height. He even managed to type out a text while up in the branches, which read: 'I don't have time to take photos using a good camera because there's an eagle around that keeps trying to attack me, and also lots of bees flying around.'

RIGHT: Maliau Basin was found accidentally by
a pilot in 1947.

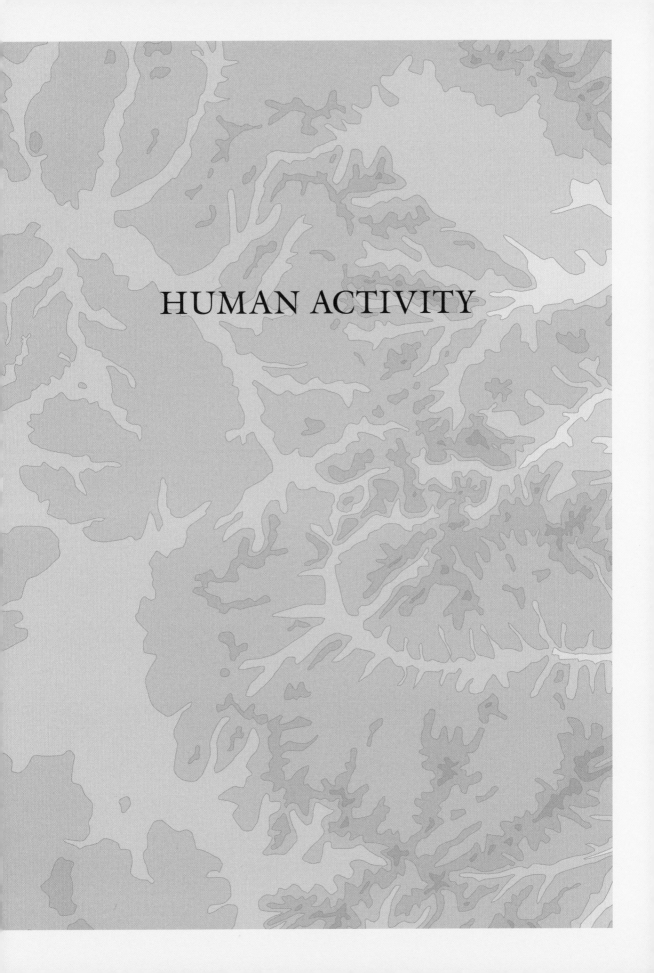

HUMAN ACTIVITY

35° 7' 53" N / 32° 44' 60" E

GREEN LINE
CYPRUS
United Nations Buffer Zone

There are plenty of striking sights that epitomise the bleak state of what were once thriving communities within the Cyprus buffer zone – nicknamed the 'Green Line'. Most famously, the rows of bird-dropping-covered seats at the old Nicosia airport and the gutted innards of an old Cyprus Airways Trident Sunjet passenger plane, gradually stripped of parts, permanently grounded outside. Slightly more low-key, yet just as poignant, are the crumbling remnants of Variseia, a village in the mountainous northwest of the island, where residents were given a single day's notice to evacuate before the area was sealed off. Here, among the empty, abandoned houses, with doors hanging from their hinges, the main residents are now a herd of mouflon – a breed of tough mountain sheep (and a national symbol of Cyprus, featuring on coins and the logo of Cyprus Airways itself). They were once close to extinction, but between 200 and 300 mouflon have since been counted living among the ruins of Variseia, and their total population within the Green Line is estimated at roughly 3,000.

Cyprus, now home to both Greek and Turkish nationals, has historically been an island of conflict, brought to a head in the years following the Republic of Cyprus's full independence in 1960. By December 1963, tensions between these two major ethnic communities had reached a stage where acts of violence began taking place across the island, culminating – as the story goes – in British Major-General Peter Young using a green pen to draw a line across a map of Cyprus, designating where a temporary buffer zone would be located to keep the two communities apart. At the time, nobody could reasonably have expected this zone to still be in place over half a century later.

The violence of 1974 became the most dramatic and pivotal clash. On 15 July, a coup d'état by forces loyal to mainland Greece took place on Cyprus, to which Turkey

responded by sending troops to storm the northern beaches, causing Greek Cypriots to flee en masse for the southern portion of the island. A ceasefire was declared a month later, but the rigid stalemate that ensued has since become the status quo. Several generations on both sides have consequently grown up in Cyprus knowing no situation other than that the island is split down the middle, with the culturally Greek Republic of Cyprus in the south, and the culturally Turkish Northern Cyprus in the north.

The Green Line – officially the United Nations Buffer Zone – runs for 110 miles across the island, and is administered by the United Nations Peacekeeping force in Cyprus (UNFICYP). The line narrows at points such as through Nicosia, which runs a semi-official slogan of being the world's last divided capital. Outside the city, however, the line widens to just over 4 miles, and overall encompasses 130 square miles, as much as 3 per cent of the island's land area. While the Green Line does include some small settlements – such as Pyla, the only village on the island where Greeks and Turks successfully live side by side as neighbours – much of the buffer zone is tightly controlled, with patrolling UNFICYP soldiers the only individuals with the authority to be in certain areas.

As well as the mouflon, plenty of wildlife has been found thriving in the relative peace of the Green Line. Extremely rare plants only found on the island have also been found in large populations, such as the Cyprus bee orchid and the Cyprus tulip. Forty years of accidental enforced protection from regular human influences has created an inadvertent nature reserve, a spot of wilderness where there could conceivably have instead been a warzone.

ABOVE: Communities in the Cyprus UN Buffer Zone have been abandoned since the 1970s.

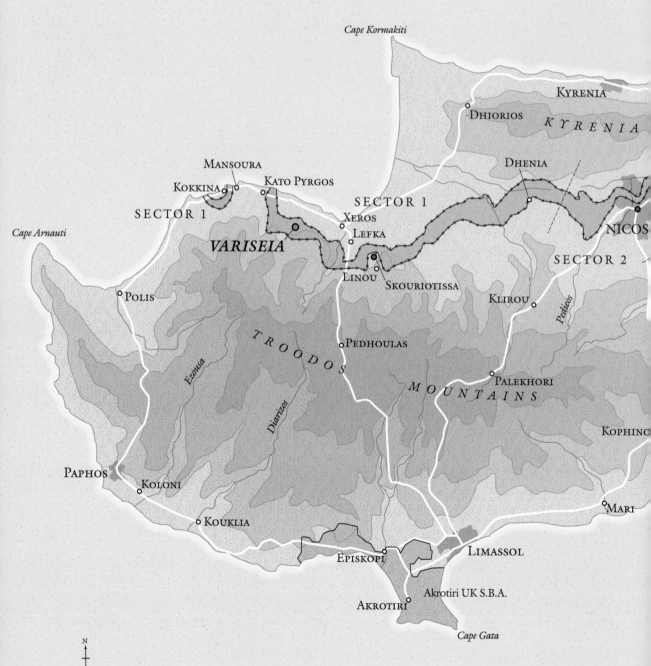

CYPRUS

Cape Kormakiti

Cape Arnauti

KYRENIA

KYRENIA

DHIORIOS

DHENIA

MANSOURA

KOKKINA

KATO PYRGOS

SECTOR 1

NICOS

SECTOR 1

XEROS

VARISEIA

LEFKA

SECTOR 2

LINOU

SKOURIOTISSA

POLIS

KLIROU

Pedieos

PEDHOULAS

TROODOS

PALEKHORI

MOUNTAINS

KOPHINO

Esousa

Diarrizos

PAPHOS

KOLONI

MARI

KOUKLIA

EPISKOPI

LIMASSOL

AKROTIRI UK S.B.A.

AKROTIRI

Cape Gata

N

Cape Andreas

RIZOKARPASO

LEONARISSO

ARDHANA

M O U N T A I N S

BOGHAZ

KYTHREA

LEFKONIKO

Pedieos

PRASTIO

FAMAGUSTA

ATHNA
(AKHNA)

Athienou

DHERINIA

SECTOR 4

PERGAMOS
PYLA

Dhekelia
UK S.B.A.

SECTOR 4

AYIA
NAPA

Cape Greco

LARNACA

M E D I T E R R A N E A N   S E A

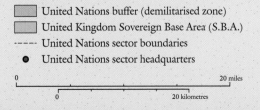

United Nations buffer (demilitarised zone)
United Kingdom Sovereign Base Area (S.B.A.)
----- United Nations sector boundaries
● United Nations sector headquarters

0   20 miles

0   20 kilometres

CHERNOBYL EXCLUSION ZONE

UKRAINE

Chernobyl

The events of 26 April 1986, when an obscure Soviet city became a household name, continue to resonate to this day. Few other place names are weighed down by history to such a magnitude. On this tragic day, one of the four reactors at the Soviet Union's Chernobyl nuclear plant, 80 miles north of Kiev, exploded, killing two people instantly. Over the following nine days, the plant emitted an immense amount of nuclear radiation – over one hundred times more than the atomic bombs dropped on Nagasaki and Hiroshima at the end of the Second World War – resulting in the deaths of several dozen more employees (exact numbers are disputed). It was the first disaster ever to hit the maximum Level 7 on the International Nuclear Event Scale (INES), matched since only by the tsunami-provoked 2011 meltdown at Fukushima, Japan.

An 18.6 miles exclusion zone was set up and local residents – as many as 336,000 people – evacuated, primarily from the nearby city of Pripyat. Nature, of course, pays scant attention to such artificial human constructs as exclusion zones. Large areas of what is now Ukraine, Belarus and Russia were contaminated by fallout in the immediate aftermath of the disaster, thanks to weather conditions blowing vast quantities of radiation in their direction. To a lesser degree, radiation from Chernobyl impacted on the environment across much of Europe, with contaminants subsequently being found in Scottish sheep, German boar and Norwegian reindeer.

Three decades later, and much of the scene on the ground looks remarkably similar to how it did in 1986. The few visitors allowed into the 1,000 square miles Chernobyl Exclusion Zone (CEZ), surrounding what is now a Ukrainian city on the border with Belarus, report post-apocalyptic scenes, a world trapped in time. Even the biological process of decomposition has ceased to operate, with research from the University of

MINSK

MOGILEV

KRICHEV

CHERIKOV

Sozh

BYKHOV

B E L A R U S

BOBRUYSK

RUSSIAN

CHACHERSK

FEDERATION

Dnieper

SLUTSK

Berezina

SOLIGORSK

VETKA

NOVOZYBKOV

GOMEL

KIMOVO

Pripyat

MOZYR

KHOINIKI

YELSK

BRAGIN

NAROWLA

OVRUCH

PRIPYAT

CHERNIGOV

NARODYCHI

CHERNOBYL

KOROSTEN

Kiev
Reservoir

Desna

NOVOGRAD VOLYNSKIY

Teteriv

KIEV

ZHITOMIR

BERDICHEV

U K R A I N E

Roska

VINNITSA

D N I E P E R

CHERKASSY

N

Curies per square km of Cesium-137

0   50 miles

0   50 kilometres

1–5   5–15   15–40   Greater than 40

South Carolina showing that the enormously high radiation levels from the accident killed off the essential topsoil bacteria and fungi required to break down organic material. Haunting remains of trees that died decades ago lie precisely where they fell, the forest floor littered with layer upon layer of dead leaves that should have long since decayed and returned their nutrients to the soil.

The settlements within the CEZ are now commonly referred to as ghost towns, empty as they are of almost any human habitation. However, that doesn't mean they are completely devoid of life. Instead, in the absence of humans, wildlife has seized upon the chance to recolonise the site and establish a firm foothold in a place we have decided we no longer wish to tread. In buildings across the city, greenery bursts from broken windows, vines crawl up walls and emerge triumphantly through rooftops. Pripyat sports stadium, where local team FC Stroitel Pripyat used to play, is now home to a mini-forest, where there was once a flat, grassy football field. The city fairground, due to open on the day of the accident, sits eerily still amid the thick wild grass.

In a challenge to our understandings about the impact of radiation on living organisms, plenty of species seem to be thriving amid the radioactive fallout. Birds in particular have shown to be far more resistant to long-term radiation-induced damage than previously hypothesised. Research conducted by scientists from the University of Portsmouth and the University of the West of England found that birds' immune systems could easily cope with radiation at levels similar to those now seen at Chernobyl. Despite warnings about shrunken brains and other such abnormalities, many bird species living on the site – such as barn swallows and great tits – show almost no signs of reacting to radiation at all.

The CEZ is now an unofficial wildlife haven, home to abundant numbers of elk and both roe and red deer. Even large mammals such as grey wolves, wild and Eurasian boars, red foxes and raccoon dogs have all been spotted – within some of the most highly contaminated areas – by camera traps set up by researchers from the University of Georgia's Savannah River Ecology Laboratory. Many of these and other species have struggled to survive in the rest of the region, as the surrounding environment has been gradually developed and urbanised, and natural habitats shrunk beyond viability.

But here, among the crumbling ruins that once symbolised the all-conquering scientific power of man, they can run free, safe from the worst impacts of human activity. Indeed, the population of wolves living in and around the CEZ is believed to be more than seven times greater than in the four uncontaminated nature reserves across the region. This is their terrain now. Despite speculation that suggests Chernobyl may be a suitable site for the construction of a solar power plant, wilderness is returning to Chernobyl, as wolves prowl through abandoned streets and deer run wild through the remains of the iconic disaster zone.

ABOVE: Since Chernobyl has become almost devoid
of humanity, it has become a haven for wildlife.

38° 19' 46" N / 127° 24' 40" E

THE DEMILITARISED ZONE
NORTH KOREA/SOUTH KOREA

Korean Peninsula

North and South Korea (officially the Democratic People's Republic of Korea and the Republic of Korea respectively) have been in a stalemate for over sixty years, since the Korean War was paused by the signing of an armistice in 1953. This ceasefire saw the drawing of a 154-mile-long line across the peninsula at the 38th parallel, a buffer zone 2½ miles wide which would become the infamous DMZ 'demilitarised zone' (in reality one of the most heavily militarised borders on the planet). Former US President Bill Clinton reportedly called the DMZ 'the scariest place on Earth'.

For over 99 per cent of the time, the face that the DMZ shows the world is one of pure, naked hostility, perfectly exhibited by the tense, stone-faced soldiers and imposing buildings staring directly at each other across the Joint Security Area. This particular spot has become famous as a space where diplomatic negotiations can take place, courtesy of the 'neutral' blue chalets that straddle both sides of the border, and is a must-stop for day-trippers visiting from the South Korean capital, Seoul.

Far from the approved stopping points of the tourist trail, however, are scenes of a place dramatically different from the stereotypical vision of the DMZ. While the land on both sides (particularly the South) has subsequently been developed and undoubtedly 'tamed' beyond recognition, the 350 square miles area of the DMZ and wider 530 square miles area of South Korea's adjacent civilian control zone (CCZ) remain essentially isolated from the outside world. The only exception remains the village of Daeseong-dong – nicknamed the 'freedom village' – and its residents, who found themselves caught on the inside when the truce was called and the borders on both sides of the DMZ became permanent. Their ancestors (the only people allowed to reside there) continue to live out their bizarre existence under the watchful eyes of the world to this day.

The other inhabitants of the DMZ/CCZ receive significantly less publicity. Thanks to this extreme isolation, the zone has an incredibly rich wild environment, with an estimated 97.4 per cent forest and grassland cover, plus vast meadows of vibrant wild flowers. Surveys have counted over 1,100 plant species, and more than 80 types of fish. Endangered black-faced spoonbills breed in large quantities on the small islands off the west coast, while 10 per cent of the world's cranes choose to winter on the central grassy Cheorwon Plain, including the vulnerable white-naped crane and the endangered red-crowned crane; the plain is one of the few remaining safe spaces for both species. At least fifty mammal species have also been confirmed in the zone, including lynx, Amur leopards, Asiatic black bears, Eurasian otters and the vulnerable water deer. Especially exciting for the people of Korea is that rumours continue to abound that there may be Siberian tigers in the DMZ. The animal is officially completely extinct in the South, yet there are numerous accounts of tiger-like footprints and tree scratches being found near the border, potential evidence that these animals are returning to a habitat where they used to roam freely.

This unique environment that has accidentally been formed within the DMZ has led to calls, both domestically and internationally, for the zone to officially become a UNESCO Biosphere Reserve, to preserve the diverse natural ecosystem. Ensuring the long-term survival of these uniquely wild ecosystems, as well as the many species living inside the buffer zone, could become the crucial cross-border diplomatic project the Korean standoff has been crying out for since the 1950s.

ABOVE: Away from the tension of the Joint Security Area, the DMZ has remained an undeveloped wilderness.

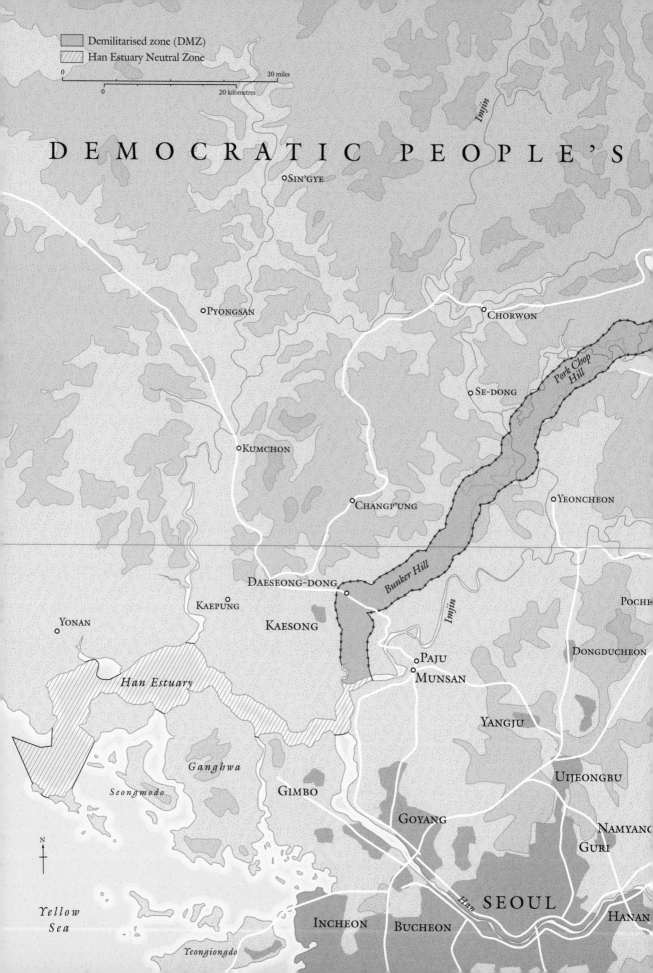

Demilitarised zone (DMZ)
Han Estuary Neutral Zone

0   20 miles

0   20 kilometres

DEMOCRATIC PEOPLE'S

Imjin

○ SIN'GYE

○ CHORWON

○ PYONGSAN

Pork Chop Hill

○ SE-DONG

○ KUMCHON

○ CHANGP'UNG

○ YEONCHEON

Bunker Hill

DAESEONG-DONG

POCH

○ KAEPUNG

KAESONG

Imjin

DONGDUCHEON

○ YONAN

Han Estuary

○ PAJU
○ MUNSAN

YANGJU

Ganghwa

GIMBO

UIJEONGBU

Seongmodo

GOYANG

NAMYANG

GURI

N

INCHEON   BUCHEON

Han

SEOUL

HANAN

*Yellow
Sea*

Yeongjongdo

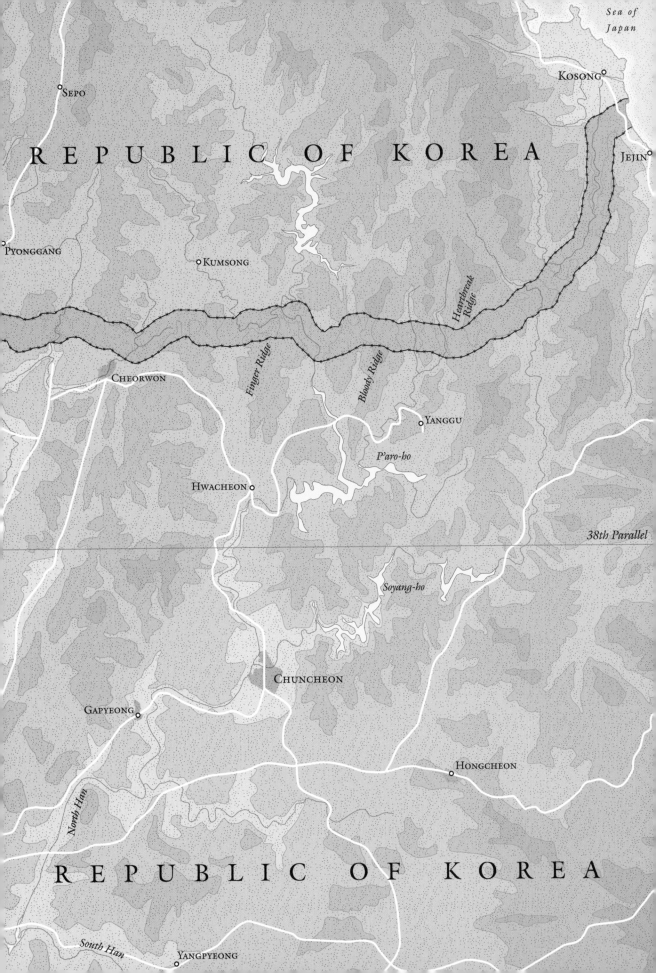

39° 50' 12" N / 104° 50' 14" W

THE ROCKY MOUNTAIN ARSENAL REFUGE

USA

Commerce City, Colorado

The Rocky Mountain Arsenal Refuge was once described as 'the most polluted square mile on Earth'. Today, however, it is a glorious, 15,000-acre monumental tribute to nature. This sanctuary of woodland, wetlands and prairie just ten miles north of Denver exudes calm and tranquillity to rival anywhere in the natural world. Clearly, its tumultuous history is quite unlike most other natural refuges.

Historically, like much of the region, the refuge started out as land for indigenous communities to herd bison and, after the arrival of European settlers, converted to cattle farms. But its life was set to take a dramatic twist in the 1940s, following the attacks on Pearl Harbor, Hawaii, which thrust the US into full-scale war. Land was quickly set aside and this part of northern America was chosen to become a chemical weapons manufacturing facility, named the Rocky Mountain Arsenal, a central location for the production and storage of nerve gas, mustard gas and napalm. After the Second World War, the call for such chemicals diminished, and the care and attention paid to the arsenal's upkeep went with it. Leased to Shell Oil, it became a site for the production of various toxic pesticides, such as dieldrin and aldrin (widely used on corn, cotton and other crops until it was banned for all usage by the Environmental Protection Agency in 1987, citing severe health hazards) as well as for Cold War-related weapons production and demilitarisation. Even the rocket fuel that carried Neil Armstrong, Buzz Aldrin and Michael Collins to the moon in Apollo 11 in July 1969 was manufactured at the Rocky Mountain Arsenal.

By the early 1980s, the facility was in severe disrepair. However, a surprising discovery was to dramatically change its fortunes. As the US Army began undertaking a clean-up of

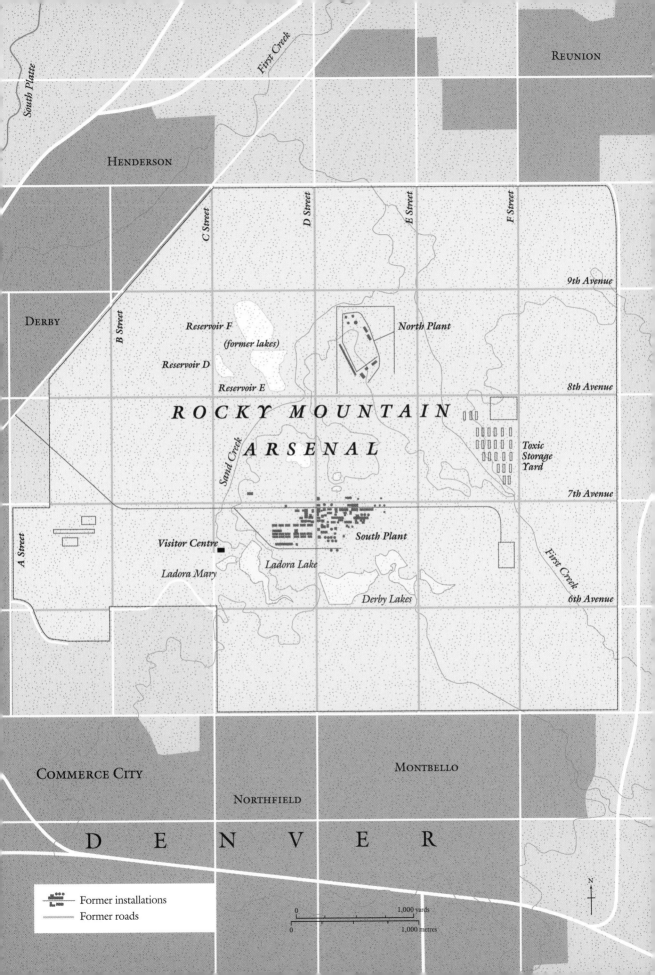

REUNION

First Creek

South Platte

HENDERSON

C Street

D Street

E Street

F Street

9th Avenue

DERBY

B Street

Reservoir F

(former lakes)

North Plant

8th Avenue

Reservoir D

Reservoir E

R O C K Y   M O U N T A I N

A R S E N A L

Sand Creek

Toxic
Storage
Yard

7th Avenue

A Street

Visitor Centre

South Plant

Ladora Mary

Ladora Lake

First Creek

6th Avenue

Derby Lakes

COMMERCE CITY

MONTBELLO

NORTHFIELD

D   E   N   V   E   R

N

Former installations

Former roads

0   1,000 yards

0   1,000 metres

the various chemicals that had leached over decades into the environment (more than 600 types of which have been detected), a roost of protected bald eagles was unexpectedly found on the site. Given the relative solitude afforded by the arsenal, the birds had always been known to roost here in winter, but over a dozen of what was then an endangered species (a status removed in 2007 – a genuine conservation success story in itself) were found in 1986. Opinions now began to change: instead of chasing them away, as had been standard practice in the past, the US Fish and Wildlife Service began conducting scientific studies. It was discovered that the eagles, known to usually enjoy a primarily fish-based diet, had developed a taste for the deceased remains of prairie dogs that inhabited the landscape. When blood tests revealed the birds to be largely unaffected by the presence of dieldrin and other chemicals, the idea of a natural refuge began to emerge.

In 1992, the United States Congress passed the Rocky Mountain Arsenal National Wildlife Refuge Act, granting protected status to the land. Consequently, in April 2004, a formal handover saw nearly 5,000 acres passed from the care of the US Army (as well as the Environmental Protection Agency and Shell) to the US Fish and Wildlife Service. 'Working together, we have transformed a vestige of the Cold War into a permanent home for bald eagles, mule deer, white pelicans and hundreds of other species of wildlife,' announced Gale Norton, Secretary for the US Department of the Interior.

Finally, in 2010, after nearly two decades, the cleaning operations concluded. Buildings once used in chemical manufacturing have all been demolished, the main chemical waste dump plugged with concrete, and all water channels flowing out of the site are now carefully treated. Controlled burns have helped remove litter, kill weeds and reinvigorate the growth of native plants, the restoration of which has seen the landscape return to the prairies that existed before being converted first to farmland and later to the chemical plant. Through planting thousands of acres of wild grasses, the newly diverse ecosystem serves as a habitat for over 330 different wildlife species, including bald eagles, bison, deer, coyotes and black-footed ferrets, and is one of the country's largest urban wildlife refuges. Although the site will in all likelihood never entirely shake it's chemical-infused past (a complete clean-up – the dedicated removal of 100 per cent of all released chemicals would have cost many billions of dollars more than the assigned $2.1 billion) it has nevertheless become a rare and highly welcome natural wild habitat for some of the country's most iconic species.

BELOW: Bison and other wildlife have recolonised the Rocky Mountain Arsenal, in the shadow of the Denver skyline.

46° 28' 57" N / 30° 43' 24" E

ODESSA CATACOMBS

Ukraine

Odessa

The port city of Odessa features a rich urban fabric of grand pastel-coloured neoclassical buildings complete with packed Black Sea beaches, cobbled promenades and cultural highlights such as the Potemkin Steps and the restored nineteenth-century opera and ballet theatre. But underground, there exists another world entirely: over 1,250 miles of dark catacombs running wild beneath the leafy city streets, a vast network which has become the final resting place for numerous doomed souls over hundreds of years.

Remarkably, the entire network is man-made, the results of two centuries of individuals taking to the world beneath the feet of their fellow citizens for various secretive and underhand activities. The catacombs were initially merely quarries for Slavic-speaking Cossacks who, following their banishment from Russia by Catherine the Great in the late eighteenth century, were accepted into this city on the banks of the Black Sea, and who required limestone to build houses. This rapidly increased the city size. As Odessa grew, taller and wider tunnels needed to be dug, so that even a horse and cart could be taken down in order to quickly and easily transport the rocks up to the surface. Decade after decade after decade of mining means they have expanded to create the tangled and essentially un-mappable labyrinth, as deep as 200 feet, that exists today. In the aftermath of the 1917 Russian revolution, this intricately wild and lawless network was later used for more nefarious means: everything from the illegal storing of wine to smuggling various products into the heavily controlled Soviet Union.

When the Second World War broke out, local resistance forces – numbering as many as 6,000 individuals – used the catacombs as a secret hideout, launching surprise night raids and sabotage attacks against the invading German and Romanian forces. So complicated is the network that, despite the vast resources of poison gas, smoke and food

Museum of
Partisan Glory

Praktychna
Harbour

Kabotazhna
Harbour

Karantynna
Harbour

N

Sofiivs'ka Street

Prymors'ka Street

Pastera Street

Primorsky Boulevard

Stambulski
Park

B L A C K

City
Garden

National
Academic
Theatre

City Hall

Preobrazhens'ka Street

Derybasivska Street

Spaso-Preobrazhensky
Cathedral

Hrets'ka Street

Kanatna Street

Nizhyns'ka Street

Novosel's'koho Street

Zhukovs'koho Street

Katerynyns'ka Street

Pushkins'ka Street

Chornomorets
Stadium

S E A

Tarasa Shevchenka
Park

O   D   E   S   S   A

Uspenska

Preobrazhens'ka Street

Starobazarnyi
Garden

Street

Bazarna Street

Velyka Arnauts'ka Street

Panteleimonivs'ka Street

Odessa Railway
Station

Kanatna Street

Starosinnyi
Square

Kulikowe
Pole
Square

Preobrazhenskyi
Park

Vodoprovidna Street

0   500 yards

0   500 metres

MOLDOVA   UKRAINE

ROMANIA

Odessa
Catacombs

Crimea

Danube

Black Sea

BULGARIA

ISTANBUL

TURKEY

blockades at their enemies' disposal, only one of the thirteen sabotage groups was ever discovered. Stories of unsuccessful reconnaissance patrols looking for these underground bases generally conclude with haunting tales of soldiers wandering in circles through the tunnels until they met their doom.

Previously, the catacombs were accessible from almost every building in Odessa, although many were sealed by the government in the 1980s. Nevertheless, they became a popular spot for spelunking teenagers keen on underground urban exploration (the so-called *podzemshchiki*), drawn by folklore promises of treasures hidden deep within the labyrinth. As well as stashes of Second World War weaponry, and famous sections of nationalist Cyrillic graffiti and poetry, there is also, randomly, a golden model of the *Titanic* supposedly hidden somewhere within the tunnels, left by a wealthy resident who happened to survive the 1912 sinking of the famous liner.

A grim and unsettling urban legend tells the disturbing story of a young woman who apparently wandered off from a New Year's Eve party in 2004 and, confused and disorientated, became fatally lost in the catacombs. When her body was eventually recovered three years later, the verdict was that it had taken several days for her to eventually die of dehydration. Whether this particular story is fiction or not, it's just one of many bodies reportedly found in the labyrinth, a narrative that says a lot about Odessa's mysterious and dangerous subterranean world.

The only 'official' access point for the catacombs now is the Museum of Partisan Glory, which documents the history of the tunnels, displaying weapons, personal belongings, photographs and documents recovered from the underground world. Beyond that, if rumours are to be believed, there are still more than a thousand access routes, both legal and illegal – making completely shutting them down almost an impossibility. Furthermore, thanks to modern-day miners who still head underground in search of limestone, the tunnels continue to grow even now, creating an ever-expanding wilderness.

ABOVE: Leftover communications equipment and other artefacts depict how the Odessa catacombs have served as a historical hideaway.

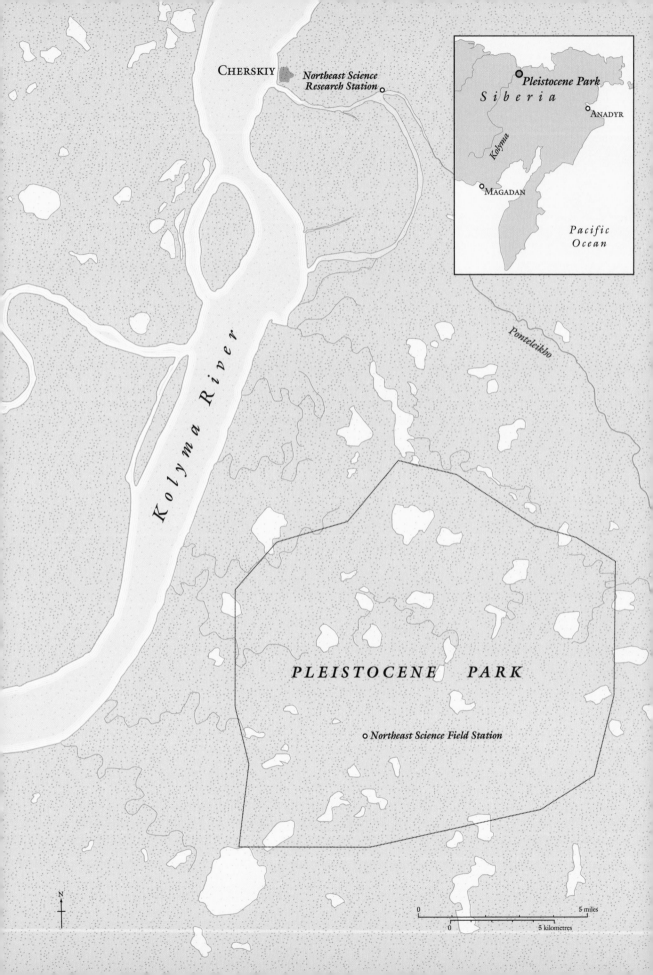

CHERSKIY

Northeast Science
Research Station

Pleistocene Park

Siberia

ANADYR

Kolyma

MAGADAN

Pacific
Ocean

Ponteleikho

Kolyma River

PLEISTOCENE   PARK

Northeast Science Field Station

N

0   5 miles

0   5 kilometres

PLEISTOCENE PARK

Russia

Northern Yakutia

Chances are, few of us would recognise the world further back in time than 12,000 years ago, the end of the last Ice Age period. At this time, the tail-end of the geological age known as the Pleistocene – landscapes that we now know to be wet, warm and vegetated, with lush, green forests and grasslands, interspersed with free-flowing rivers and lakes – would instead have been trapped in a deep freeze. From Europe and across the Eurasian continent, over the Bering Strait and into North America, the standard environment would overwhelmingly have been what is known as permafrost, when low temperatures froze the ground solid, and enormous glaciers spread far and wide across the surface. Across most of the planet – with a few exceptions – this is an environment that has ceased to exist in our world.

We humans – *Homo sapiens* – evolved during the Pleistocene years, although it wasn't until the following geological age, the Holocene, that we found warmer climatic conditions under which we could truly thrive. As this brave new world allowed us to start migrating across the planet, some humans headed north, where they found megafauna – mammoths and woolly rhinoceroses – stranded in the frozen tundra of the far northern hemisphere, the only remaining ecosystem in which these cold-adapted animals could survive. When the Pleistocene had come to an end, and the wide-ranging permafrost habitat that had once stretched almost all the way around the globe disappeared, mammoths and other iconic Pleistocene animals found themselves trapped at the very top of the world, on places such as the vast barren landmass of the Taimyr Peninsula, or remote Wrangel Island off the northern coast of Siberia, deep inside the Arctic Circle, where freezing polar vortex temperatures kept the regional climate cold enough for them. Unfortunately, the immigrating humans had no problem cornering and killing off those

few animals who had somehow survived the geological shift. Thanks to the hand of man,
the Pleistocene era megafauna came to a dramatic and bloody end.

While the permafrost environment may not exist on the grand scale it once did during
the Pleistocene, the fact that places do still exist where these conditions persist into the
twenty-first century (primarily northern Siberia, Alaska and Canada's Yukon territory)
presents us with the opportunity to learn from this long-distant geological time. In fact,
if you head deep into northern Siberia, to roughly three miles from the town of Chersky,
you'll find a place where a quite extraordinary experiment is taking place.

They call it Pleistocene Park. In this sixty square miles area – where extremely low-
temperature conditions have maintained a frozen environment not unlike that of the
Pleistocene era, divided evenly between meadow, forest and willow shrubland – wild
animals such as bison, moose, musk oxen, reindeer and wild Yakutian horses roam free,
joined by predators such as wolves, lynx, wolverines and bears, all uninhibited by the
interfering actions of humanity. The prosperity of these and other wildlife which can
comfortably survive in such conditions is actively encouraged, in order to try and recreate
the ancient permafrost ecosystem, by reintroducing as much ancient wildlife as possible,
and continuing to expand the land available for this remarkable experiment.

It all stems from the ambitious vision of Sergey Zimov, a geophysicist who is
director of the Northeast Science Station in Chersky, the Republic of Sakha, Russia. He
began studying extinctions in this part of the world in the early 1980s, but soon found

himself yearning to do something more pioneering, more daring. Towards the end of the 1980s, Zimov decided to act, and began setting land aside for the specially reconstituted Pleistocene Park, his grand project.

The largest of the Pleistocene megafauna may be gone forever, but Zimov aims to otherwise recreate the environment as closely as possible, perhaps even one day hosting and protecting rare Siberian tigers, a species whose numbers were once as low as twenty to thirty in the 1930s, but have since dramatically recovered to as many as four hundred individuals.

Why do all of this? Mere conservation-led habitat restoration aside, Zimov emphasises the key role that melting permafrost is likely to have in escalating highly damaging human-induced climate change. Vast quantities of greenhouse gases such as carbon dioxide and methane have been trapped within the frozen tundra for thousands of years (two to three times more than is stored within the planet's rainforests). As the climate warms, the permafrost is melting, and these gases are escaping in ever-larger quantities, thereby aiding more warming and more melting – a vicious circle. Studies have suggested that the presence of large grazing animals compacts the snow-covered tundra, exposing the ground to cold temperatures, thereby reducing ice-melt and limiting methane loss. Zimov hopes that maintaining as much of the wild Pleistocene-like permafrost landscape he has created as possible will help stave off the worst impacts of climate change. The return of this long-distant environment could yet have a pivotal role to play in protecting the planet for millennia.

CENTRALIA
USA

Pennsylvania

The air is thick with the pungent scent of sulphur, as though infused with rotten eggs. Thin columns of dense black smoke erupt with gusto through jagged lacerations in the road, where the tarmac has been literally ripped apart. In every direction, the ghostly foundations of small-town America crisscross the landscape, the disused street signs and empty, overgrown driveways now faint whispers of what was once upon a time a perfectly ordinary Appalachian mountain town. Welcome to Centralia, Pennsylvania, a place the legendary travel writer Bill Bryson described in his book *A Walk in the Woods* as 'the strangest, saddest town I believe I have ever seen'.

Councillors in Centralia could never have imagined the series of events they would set in motion when, so the story goes, they met on 7 May 1962 to discuss several local matters, including clearing up the new local landfill site. The site in question had, until a few months previously, been on a strip-mine pit for excavating coal, 300ft long, 75ft wide and at least 50ft deep. Now completely abandoned, it was the logical choice for locals to use for landfill. Normal practice for clean-up operations was simple: set it on fire, thereby burning off excess waste, flushing out rats, and generally taking control of the site.

On Sunday 27 May, a hired team congregated at the pit, someone lit a match, and the fire began. The assembled firemen watched as it burned through all the debris on the surface, then, once it had successfully cleared much of the visible waste, they began pouring water on the smouldering flames. As the smoke died down, they packed up and went home, another job well done.

Two days later, a passer-by spotted black smoke emerging from the landfill. The alarm was raised, and local people gathered to spend several hours, deep into the night, spraying jets of water onto the rejuvenated fire, attempting to halt it in its tracks.

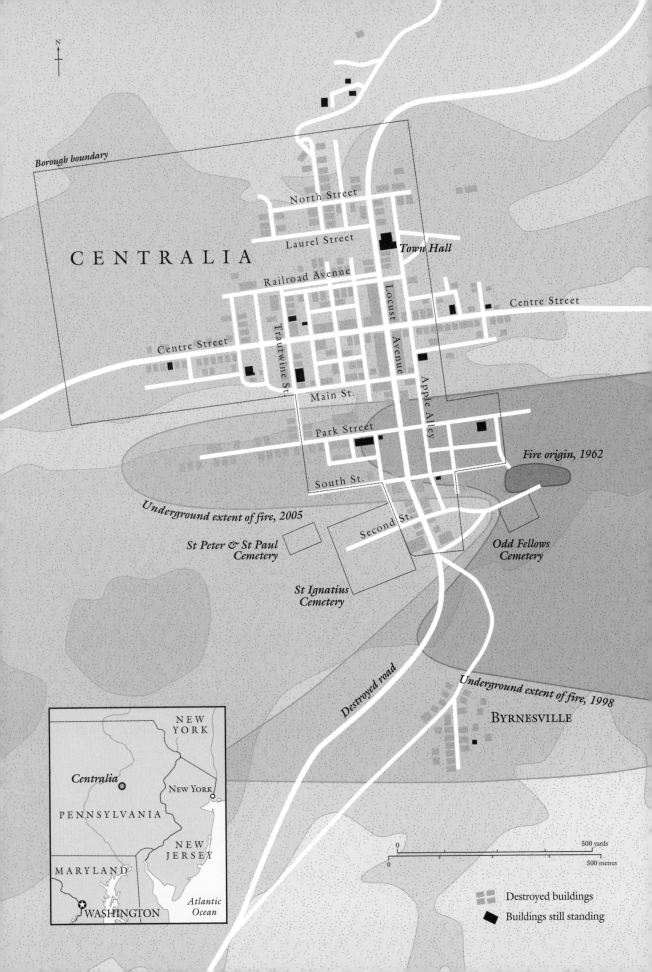

N

CENTRALIA

Borough boundary

North Street

Laurel Street

Railroad Avenue

Town Hall

Locust Avenue

Centre Street

Centre Street

Trautwine St.

Main St.

Apple Alley

Park Street

Fire origin, 1962

South St.

Underground extent of fire, 2005

St Peter & St Paul
Cemetery

Second St.

Odd Fellows
Cemetery

St Ignatius
Cemetery

Destroyed road

Underground extent of fire, 1998

BYRNESVILLE

NEW
YORK

Centralia

NEW YORK

PENNSYLVANIA

NEW
JERSEY

MARYLAND

*Atlantic
Ocean*

WASHINGTON

0   500 yards

0   500 metres

Destroyed buildings

Buildings still standing

Despite their best efforts, this was unsuccessful, and for several days the pit continued to smoulder, emitting a foul stench into the air. Although plugging pits to prevent flames spreading has always been a priority when conducting planned landfill fires, it turned out that one fairly sizeable hole at the base of the pit, roughly 15ft long, had been missed. Consequently, this unplugged hole had operated as a convenient escape route for the fire, which had successfully tunnelled through into Pennsylvania's old anthracite coal network, and set it ablaze. By the summer, despite various efforts to halt the fire's progress, a mine fire was officially declared.

For nearly two decades, the town faced the constant threat of this mine fire lingering in the background to everything they did. When initial efforts at flushing it out were terminated due to bad weather and a lack of funds, the estimated costs of tackling the blaze began skyrocketing into millions of dollars, preventing anyone or any organisation from taking meaningful action. Ultimately, with few solutions on the table, this great roaring fire running wild beneath the mountainside somehow managed to fall off the public radar.

On 14 February 1981, Centralia hit national headlines. Twelve-year old Todd Domboski was playing in his grandmother's back garden when he noticed a strange wisp of smoke coming out of the ground. Walking over to investigate, he suddenly felt the

ground completely give way beneath his feet. Swinging out an arm, he grabbed hold of some exposed roots, and found himself dangling on the precipice of a giant sinkhole, up to 4ft across and over 100ft deep. Thankfully for young Domboski, such an event doesn't happen without people noticing, and passers-by quickly rushed over to pull him to safety.

While that event alone might not have been terminal for the town, a month later, John Coddington, former mayor of Centralia, had to be stretchered to hospital after his home became filled by carbon monoxide one evening, nearly poisoning him and his family in their sleep. With such a dangerous threat to every resident lurking beneath their feet, the decision was made to evacuate the entire town. Roughly one thousand residents lived in the town at the turn of the 1980s, when plans were put into place to move them all as quickly as possible. Centralia became a toxic wasteland, the mere remnants of an abandoned ghost town.

Not all residents left. At the last count, there were seven residents who continue, for one reason or another, to insist on still living in Centralia. In October 2013, the seven won a court case granting them the right to live out the rest of their lives there, after which their properties, like the rest in this once-lively town, will fall under the ownership of officials, and become condemned, and ultimately demolished. Experts estimate there is enough coal underground to keep the fire burning for over a thousand years.

WEIRD WORLDS

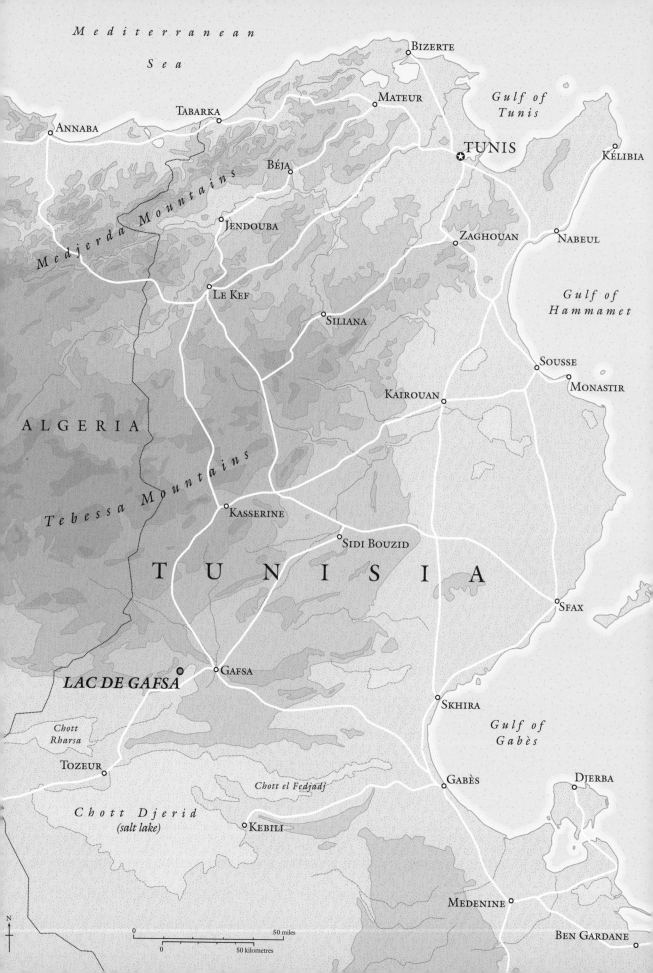

LAC DE GAFSA

TUNISIA

Gafsa

'Gafsa is miserable,' run the lines of an ancient Arab song. 'Its water is blood, its air is poison. You may live there a hundred years without making a friend.'

Despite this negative assessment, roughly 110,000 people currently call Gafsa, in the uplands of central Tunisia, home. Nevertheless, Gafsa is, to put it mildly, a fairly intense place to live. A century ago, Edwardian explorer Norman Douglas visited the town and was considerably unimpressed, describing 'bleak mountains' and 'fierce shiftings of temperature . . . nocturnal radiation that splits the very rocks and renders life impossible for many plants'.

From the winter's 'intense cold' – often approaching freezing – to summer temperatures stuck for several months at over 40°C (110°F), when monthly rainfall can be so infrequent as to be considered essentially absent (as little as 1mm/0.04in in the whole of July), Gafsa is certainly a place of extremes. Local residents, therefore, could hardly be blamed for occasionally seeing mirages during the middle of summer. What could be more appealing, amid the epic summer heat, than the opportunity to take a refreshing swim in a vast desert swimming pool?

Remarkably, in July 2014, such a vision suddenly became a reality. One day, local shepherds returned from the desert with scarcely believable tales of a lake that had mysteriously emerged from the sand overnight, at a site 15 miles west of Gafsa. Word spread fast, and when curious locals arrived at the spot, they weren't disappointed. As promised, where there were once dry, arid sand dunes, there was now a large lake, with a reported depth of between 30 and 60 feet. Naturally, the Lac de Gafsa became an instant tourist hotspot, as residents flocked to see this mysterious phenomenon and relax in its cooling waters.

So where did the lake come from? How does such an unlikely landmark appear in the middle of a sandy desert? The exact details remain sketchy, but it is no coincidence that Gafsa was historically known as an oasis town. The 'tangle of palms that sweep southward in a radiant trail of green' was one of the few elements of the town to receive any kind words of acknowledgement from Norman Douglas. More than 5,000 acres of land around Gafsa comprise the contemporary oasis, with olive trees, apricot trees, pomegranate trees and date palms growing in abundance, thanks to the natural water sources flowing beneath the surface and irrigating the land.

To add to Gafsa's unique geological background, it also happens to be the focal point of Tunisia's phosphate mining industry, and has been since the late nineteenth century, when the country was still under French control. Tunisia is now the world's fifth-highest exporter of phosphate, making it the country's number one international export. A logical outcome from this situation was therefore to assume that the water of Lac de Gafsa must be contaminated with phosphate. This is exactly the conclusion local authorities came to, especially when the water suddenly turned from crystal clear to a murky green. They

warned that the water could in fact be carcinogenic, even radioactive, and that people should stay well away from it for their own health. Their concerns are not dissimilar to what has been reported in the Gulf of Gabes, on Tunisia's east Mediterranean coast, where industrial waste by-products from phosphate processing are believed to have poisoned the water, killing vast fish populations and decimating the local fishing industry.

Typically, many people did the exact opposite of what they were advised, and instead continued to arrive in droves for a swim in Gafsa's 'Mysterious Lake'. 'Some say it is a miracle, while others are calling it a curse,' one reporter described to France 24. While a few people may have chosen to avoid the contaminants potentially contained within the strange, stagnant waters of Lac de Gafsa, government health warnings continued to fall on deaf ears. The only certainty regarding the peculiar circumstances surrounding this remote and mysterious Tunisian lake is that it is, indeed, mysterious.

BELOW: The Lac de Gafsa suddenly emerged in the middle of the desert.

MODO ISLAND
South Korea
Hoedong

Jindo Island, off the southern coast of the mainland of the Korean peninsula, is, at 140 square miles, the third largest of South Korea's 3,400 islands, and is commonly known in the country for a couple of unusual reasons. Firstly, it is the spiritual home for *Jindotgae*, the 'Jin Island dog', a short hunting canine with thick, white fur and a distinctive arched tail, which is officially protected as a national monument. However, this alone does not account for the hundreds of thousands of people who flock here each year.

Instead, we have to look to an old Korean folk tale. As the story goes, once upon a time, there were many tigers living on Jindo. Initially, the residents of the coastal village of Hoedong were able to live alongside the tigers. However, they eventually all decided to flee to nearby Modo Island for safety. Sadly, through an unfortunate mix-up, one old lady, Grandma Bbyong, was left behind and ended up stranded in the village by herself. Determined not to give up and accept this life of loneliness, she prayed daily to Yongwang, the god of the ocean, asking to be with her family again. One day, a true miracle occurred: the sea between Jindo and Modo separated, and a clear path appeared, glistening in the sunlight, inviting Bbyong to walk along it. She followed the path, and it took her all the way to Modo, dramatically reuniting her with her family.

At first glance, Modo is entirely unremarkable, and for most of the year it is treated as such; an obscure, secluded island surrounded by fast-swirling currents and unpredictable whirlpools, the stretch of water between Modo and Jindo rippling gently with sea breezes blowing in from where the Yellow and East China seas meet. Occasionally, however, this remote corner becomes inundated with tourists, as hundreds of thousands head over from the mainland to witness a bizarre phenomenon.

JINDO ISLAND

Hoedong

seasonal low tide sandbar

Geumhodo Island

Geumhodo Village

Modo Island

Modo Village

SEA OF JAPAN

N

| 0 | | 200 yards |
| 0 | | 200 metres |

The distance between Modo and the beach Hoedong-ri on neighbouring Jindo covers a distance of roughly 1.8 miles of deep and restless seawater. And yet, twice a year, the tide recedes so far that the water becomes shallow enough to wade through. Eventually – for a brief hour – a 130ft-wide sandbar emerges from the sea, an entire stretch of the seabed exposed to the air. This strange occurrence has, not unsurprisingly, led to it being known, among other names, as a 'Moses Miracle'. More commonly, it carries the name the 'Miracle Sea Road'. Naturally, such a phenomenon is a huge draw for tourists, and this dry passageway increasingly attracts huge crowds to undertake the iconic walk between Modo and Jindo (and back again, if they are quick enough). At its busiest, the narrow walkway becomes packed with up to half a million attendees at a time, all walking – or perhaps more accurately queuing – to experience this peculiar geographical quirk. Stranded clams, octopi, seaweed and other seafood can even be picked up by passers-by as they walk past.

For those who prefer a slightly more robust, scientific explanation for such phenomena than the prayers of a lonely old lady, the appearance of the Miracle Sea Road can be explained by a theory known as tidal harmonics. First devised by Britain's acclaimed Lord Kelvin (Sir William Thomson) in 1867, the theory factors in the multiple influences on the world's tides (such as the relative positions of the earth, sun and moon) to reveal predictable patterns. Occasionally, all these different influences will combine to create an exceptionally high or low tide. Thanks to the particularly low depth of the seabed between Modo and Jindo, such an extreme low tide exposes this channel entirely, and the Miracle Sea Road comes into existence.

Eventually, it became impossible for people to regularly congregate at this location without a fully fledged festival breaking out. Hence, the annual Miracle Sea Road Festival was born, a showcase for the island's cultural traditions and local talent, including folk plays, music and dancing. It features such highlights as a dawn walk along the passageway complete with fire torches, and a prayer service at the special shrine to Grandma Bbyong, memorialising her legendary status among festival goers. Despite the weight of scientific evidence behind the bizarre appearance of the Miracle Sea Road, it is the story of Grandma's Bbyong's prayers to Yongwang which remains the popular narrative of choice in this part of the world.

RIGHT: The seasonal emerging of the Miracle
Sea Road is a major attraction, drawing
crowds of thousands.

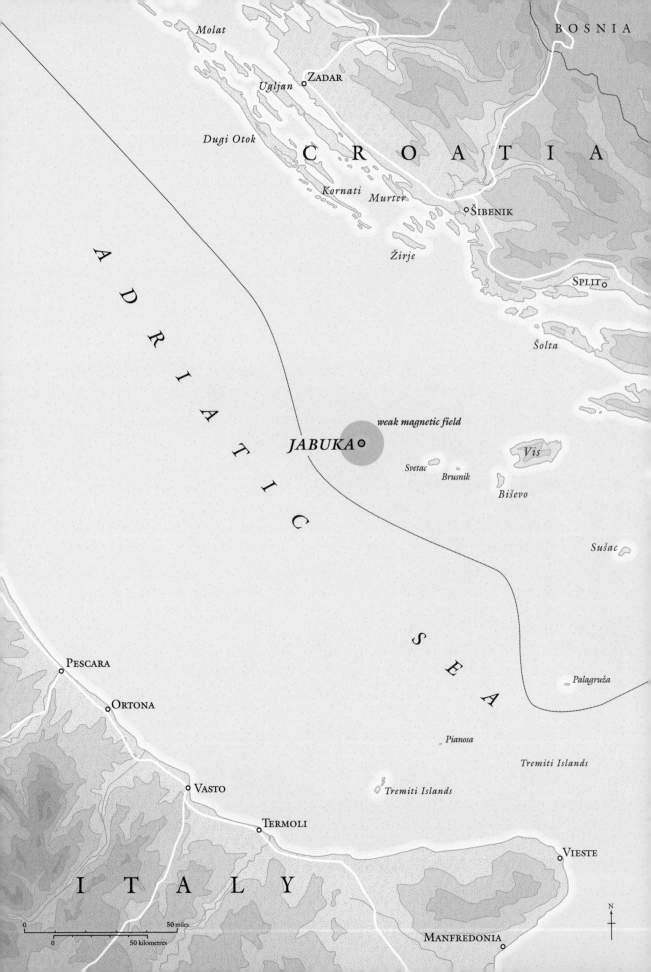

JABUKA

CROATIA

Adriatic Sea

Historically, maritime sailors would have been quite literally lost without the ability to use the earth's natural magnetism to navigate their way around the globe. Even as GPS and other modern technologies become ubiquitous, the humble compass is still the tool of choice for many smaller vessels, such as those that crisscross between tiny island chains in the Mediterranean. Woe betide any sailor, therefore, who passes through the Adriatic Sea and dares get too close to Jabuka, the region's infamous 'magnetic island'.

The peak of a submerged volcano that emerges through the surface of the water, Jabuka appears like a dark beacon on the horizon, a small, cone-shaped igneous islet sandwiched between the deep blue of the sea below and the bright sky above. It has frequently been compared to everything from a large pine cone to the Great Pyramids of Egypt to, strangely, an apple (a comparison that has certainly proved popular one way or another, since Jabuka translates to 'apple' in Croatian). Together with its neighbours Brusnik and Svetac, it forms part of Croatia's over 1,000-strong Dalmatian archipelago.

However, Jabuka is also known as the spot in the eastern Mediterranean where compasses begin to act somewhat strangely. The island consists almost entirely of volcanic magnetite, rich with iron ore, which is sufficiently strong to override the normal magnetic force of the earth, causing chaos for maritime navigators. So strong is the magnetic field emitted from the island, passing compasses cease pointing north, and instead find themselves turning haywire, losing direction under the influence of the island's magnetic pull. It is one side effect of the general instability of the whole region, which is also susceptible to frequent earthquakes. The whole Croatian coast between the cities of Zadar and Split is vulnerable to seismic shocks, with more than a thousand microquakes per year, thanks to the ongoing movement of the restless Jabuka-Andrija fault system.

As if all this is not good enough reason to follow the example set by experienced sailors in the region and avoid the island's sphere of influence, actually trying to set foot on Jabuka is an ill-advised challenge in itself. This is thanks to the very deep water around the island – which prevents boats from dropping anchor – and the steep rocky cliffs that rise impressively towards the sky. Reaching 300ft high, Jabuka is completely uninhabited (and essentially uninhabitable), home to only a handful of wild creatures, such as the hardy Dalmatian wall lizard and a population of small Norwegian lobster (scampi) that live in the surrounding coral reefs.

That's not to say that people haven't repeatedly made treacherous visits to the island. Many historical records from merchants and travellers passing through the Adriatic frequently mention the unique shape of Jabuka looming out of the ocean towards them (calling it everything from 'Melisella' to 'Millo' to 'Pomo', creating understandable confusion among mapmakers). Crucially, a significant number also commented upon the enormous numbers of falcons that swooped up and down upon the island. Falcon hunting consequently became a very popular activity on Jabuka; people would sail out to the island, clamour across this tiny rocky outcrop and risk their lives in the hope of catching a bird or two which they could take back and sell on the mainland. Dangerous as this source of income undoubtedly was, the potential rewards were considered worth the risk; a handsome profit could be made by selling such birds to wealthy customers in Italy, Germany or France. Jacques La Saige, a sixteenth-century French cloth and silk merchant, records in his journal a story he was told of four poor individuals who arrived on Jabuka in 1516 with their eyes set on the riches a captured falcon would bring them. Unfortunately, they failed to secure their boat properly, and an unexpected storm broke it free, leaving the group forced to watch it drift away into the Adriatic. With no food or water with them, and no potential search party waiting for them to return, all four tragically perished on the island's inhospitable terrain.

The island's quirky characteristics – particularly its isolation and distinctive shape – now act as a key landmark for the annual Jabuka boat race, when vessels challenge each other to sail from Vodice harbour on the Croatian coast straight out into the Adriatic, towards Italy, before turning around at Jabuka and returning to the starting point. It's a round trip of 90 miles – assuming they don't get lost en route, of course.

ABOVE: Jabuka emits its own weak magnetic field, enough to confuse passing compasses.

10° 1' 40" N / 71° 34' 37" W

LAKE MARACAIBO

VENEZUELA

Maracaibo

The dying days of the Venezuelan War of Independence – when the Spanish Empire lost control of one of its South American jewels – centred on Lake Maracaibo, at the mouth of the Catatumbo River, northwest Venezuela. In July 1823, pro-independence republican forces commanded by Admiral José Prudencio Padilla clashed in the lake with Spanish ships led by Captain Ángel Laborde. If Venezuelan legend is to be believed, this moment in history was set to pivot on a bizarrely violent act of nature.

As Padilla and his squadron sat in the lake, Laborde ordered his ships to subtly manoeuvre into an attack formation. Under cover of darkness, they began to sneak from the open sea into the lake, intending to take Padilla and the republicans by surprise. However, the invading armada were set to have their plan dramatically interrupted. Bright light began to rip across the night sky, illuminating Lake Maracaibo as if it were the middle of the day. It immediately gave away the positions of the Spanish ships, terminating their tactical advantage. Padilla ordered his forces to retaliate, and succeeded in defeating almost the entire Spanish fleet: seizing several ships, capturing or killing hundreds of men, and driving the final nail into Spanish efforts to resist the takeover of their American colonies by pro-independence forces.

What was this phenomenon, which so scuppered Laborde's attempted assault? According to local storytellers, it was a particularly dramatic incidence of what is commonly known as the Catatumbo lightning, thousands of lightning bolts striking the water every hour, the so-called 'everlasting storm'. At 93 miles long by 68 miles wide, Lake Maracaibo is the largest lake in South America (assuming it is accepted as a lake, as opposed to a tidal inlet, in which case Lake Titicaca in the Andes becomes the continent's largest), and it receives more lightning strikes on average than any other single location

in the world. With as many as 28 per minute for up to 300 nights each year, a total of roughly 1.2 million strikes annually, it sits ahead of the high-altitude village of Kifuka, in the Democratic Republic of Congo, and the Brahmaputra Valley in East India. The storm, which peaks during the wet season in August and September and is calmest around January and February, can be seen for hundreds of miles, an unmistakable flare in the sky. At the beginning of the nineteenth century, the iconic German explorer and naturalist Alexander von Humboldt described how navigators would use these electrical storms as a guide, dubbing it 'The lighthouse of Maracaibo'.

The phenomenon, which sees each square mile of the lake hit by over 500 lightning bolts each year, is generally believed to be caused by the clash between hot air blowing in from the tropical Caribbean Sea and cool air descending from the snowy Andes. Trapped on all sides by the steep slopes of the Maracaibo basin, which reach as high as 12,000ft, the warm, moist air is pushed higher and higher, forming dense, towering cumulonimbus clouds reaching as high as 30,000–40,000ft directly upwards. Within the clouds, collusions between the two air masses builds up an increasingly powerful charge of static electricity. The result is a regular explosion of climatic electricity night after night, creating quite a spectacle for the region's toucans, iguanas, alligators, howler monkeys, jaguars, boa constrictors and other exotic forest wildlife.

Alternative theories have suggested that lightning strikes are attracted by uranium deposits in the bedrock, or even that the air in the basin is more electrically conductive due to the significant quantities of methane emitted by the oil that lurks below the lake (around two-thirds of Venezuela's exported oil goes through Lake Maracaibo). Indigenous Bari legend describes how the light is created by a concentration of millions of fireflies. Whatever the reason, the lightning is so emblematic that a lightning bolt has even made its way onto the flag of Zulia, the province of which Maracaibo is the capital, alongside the blue of Lake Maracaibo's waters, the black of Zulia's oil wealth, and the warm golden sun. '*La luz con el relámpago, tenaz del Catatumbo, del nauta fija el rumbo, cual límpido farol,*' croons the Zulia regional anthem *Himno de Zulia*, 'Riding the Waves', which translates as 'Alight with lightning, the tenacious Catatumbo, the traveller sets the course, like a clear lantern.' The Catatumbo lightning is more than just a weather phenomenon; it forms an entire identity embraced by the Venezuelan people in this most extraordinary of locations.

LEFT: Epic lightning storms are a frequent sight at
Lake Maracaibo.

QIANTANG RIVER

CHINA

Hangzhou

The year was 1888, and British Commander William Moore was in charge of HMS *Rambler*, on duty in the British colonies of the Far East, principally Hong Kong. One day, he and his crew were called upon to investigate a peculiar phenomenon that had been reported on the Qiantang, a river which flows through the modern city of Hangzhou, 105 miles southwest of Shanghai, and emerges into the East China Sea. He had received word of strange tidal surges powering their way up the river estuary, leaving chaos in their wake, surges which the locals blamed on a murder that had occurred over a millennium earlier, in which the body had been thrown into the river.

Moore and the *Rambler* arrived on site and waited for the phenomenon to occur. While the junks and other traditional Chinese sailing ships used by local villagers were tightly secured to elevated platforms high above the water level, Moore scoffed at the idea that such a wide river channel could ever grow to such a significantly increased height, and ordered a handful of small boats out onto the river to survey the surge as it took place. To his shock, a sudden torrent caused the water level to increase by as much as nine feet in just ten minutes, causing major difficulties for all his boats. It turned out the locals knew exactly what they were doing, moving their boats far out of harm's way.

The entrance of a tidal bore is a dramatic and astounding sight. From a calm surface gently rippling in the breeze, a complete wall of water can be observed charging upstream with immense power, washing away everything in its path. No matter how many warnings are issued about the unpredictable nature of such phenomena, people continue to be caught out by the raw power they can sustain, especially in vast wide river mouths such as the Qiantang.

Essentially, tidal bores occur when a full or new moon exerts an exceptionally powerful gravitational pull on the ocean, creating an especially high tide and sending a single huge wave up the channel. In southwest England, the Severn River witnesses probably the most well-studied of all the world's tidal bores, and frequently draws a crowd of eager spectators. They are found in at least eighty locations around the world, generally wherever wide river channels combine with high tidal ranges. Hence, the biggest in the world are the Pororoca, which powers its way up the Amazon from the Atlantic Ocean, and, of course, Qiantang. The unique triangular shape of the shallow Qiantang estuary, and the way it rapidly narrows from as wide as 62 miles to a mere 2 miles across, acts as a funnel to amplify the effect of the tidal bore, hence creating the largest in the whole world.

It is certainly quite the occasion in Hangzhou – now a city of over six million people – when the tidal bore comes to town, where it is known as the 'Silver Dragon'. The event can be predicted with amazing accuracy, always around the eighteenth day of the eighth month of the lunar calendar, placing it in September or October, during the Mid-Autumn Festival. Huge crowds, thousands strong, congregate in Hangzhou and the nearby town of Yanguan, lining the metal fences and concrete walls along the river, to witness the famous event; a wall of water charging up from the sea at up to 25 miles per hour, powering past skyscrapers and huge bridges, submerging small walkways and roads as it goes. It's an extremely popular spot among the surfing community, drawing ambitious individuals from around the world for a chance to show off their skills while riding this powerful surge. However, year after year, the event makes headlines for stories of people being injured and sometimes even killed, having underestimated the speed, power and reach of the wave, just like Moore did over a century ago.

ABOVE: The world's largest tidal bore produces a powerful surge of water in Hangzhou, China.

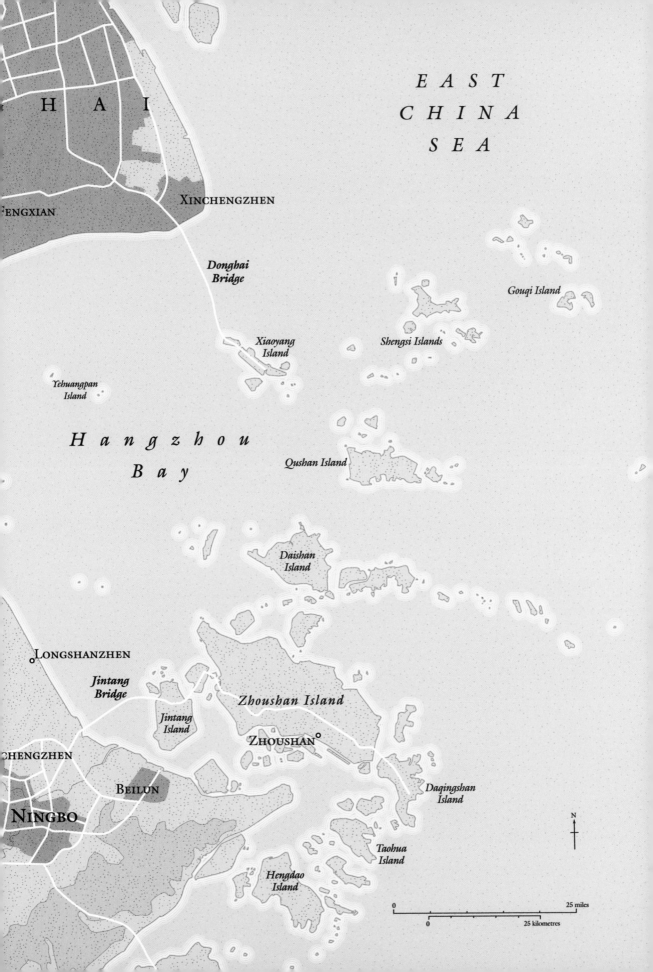

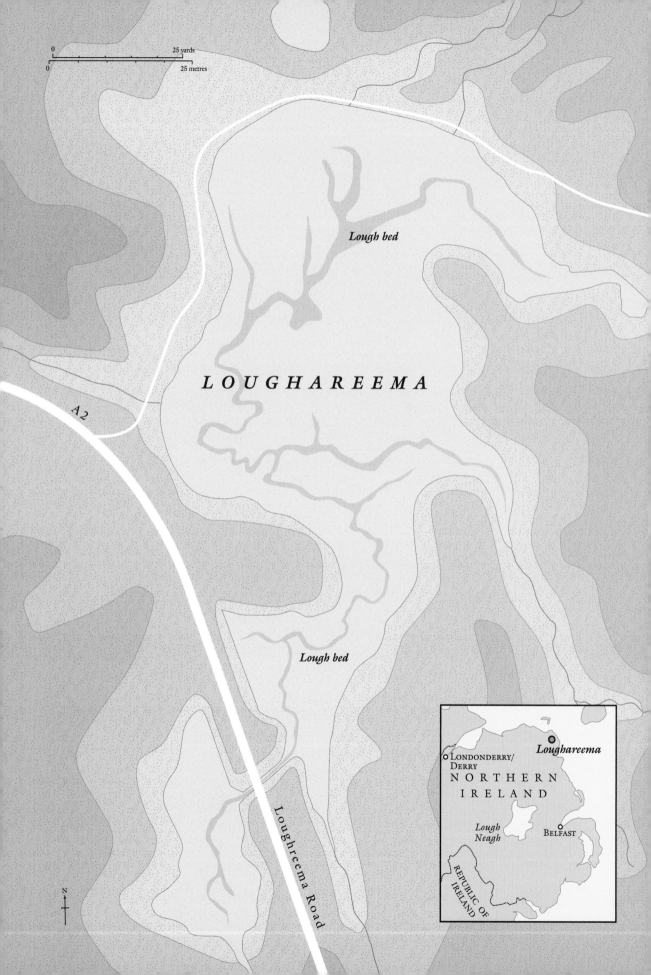

0   25 yards

0   25 metres

Lough bed

L O U G H A R E E M A

A2

Lough bed

Loughreema Road

N

○ LONDONDERRY/
DERRY

◉ *Loughareema*

N O R T H E R N
I R E L A N D

*Lough
Neagh*

○ BELFAST

REPUBLIC OF
IRELAND

LOUGHAREEMA
NORTHERN IRELAND, UK
Ballycastle

Colonel John Magee McNeill had a train to catch. The date was 30 September 1898, and he had been staying with his cousin Captain Daniel McNeill in Cushendun, on the northeast coast of Northern Ireland. At 1 p.m., he left by horse-drawn cart to his destination of Ballycastle, roughly 12 miles away, from where he would catch the 3 p.m. train. Unfortunately, it had been raining heavily for the previous few days, and the road had become submerged underwater in parts, to the degree that many other travellers had opted not to travel that day, instead deciding to wait for the water to recede. Around halfway through the journey, the cart passed a lake known locally for rising and falling rapidly with the weather. On this occasion, it had risen so dramatically high that, halfway through wading through the flood, the horses refused to budge any further. Despite the best efforts of the coachman, he couldn't get the horses to move. One of the horses, spooked by the surrounding waters, took fright and reared up on its hind legs. As it brought its legs back down, it landed off to the side of the highway, and slipped off the road itself. Suddenly, both horses were falling into the lake, dramatically hauling the entire carriage off the road and dooming both the coachman and his passenger.

Welcome to the deceptive 'Vanishing Lake', officially named Loughareema, which crudely translates in Gaelic as 'water ran out'. Where once the road which McNeill was travelling along ran straight through the lake basin, making it passable only when water levels were low, the modern A2 road is raised up on a causeway, making such distressingly dramatic accidents far less prone to occur. Yet the phenomenon that took McNeill's carriage by surprise continues to the present day. The depth of this relatively small lake can vary wildly, from a state of being essentially completely empty to as large as 20ft deep and 1,300ft long. After heavy rains – to which this region is certainly prone

– at least three streams flash-flow over highly impermeable rock and quickly empty into the lake, filling it in as little as twelve to eighteen hours.

Peat deposits mean this water is very unclear; a hand dipped into the water can become impossible to view as soon as it is below the surface. In turn, when the rain has ended, the water can vanish entirely over four to six days, leaving little trace of its existence. A camera set up by the Geological Survey of Northern Ireland, which documented the lake's changing level over ten months in 2015, now allows us to watch a time-lapse of the lake filling and emptying, filling and emptying, over and over and over again. There is an odd satisfaction that comes from switching between the two series of photographs taken three years apart by Google's Streetview cars when passing the lake, which display it in both its full and empty state – one showing an entirely empty basin, the other revealing the car to in fact be in the middle of a swollen lake on both sides of the road. Crucially, however, there are no rivers or streams of any kind flowing out of the lake. This poses a number of significant questions – namely, why does the water level fluctuate as it does and, when it empties, where does the water go?

The answer appears to lie in a cone-shaped sinkhole located in the base of the lake, through which water can flow, although at a limited rate. When the amount of water entering the basin exceeds that which can escape through the sinkhole, the lake fills. As soon as the rate of water drops, then the level of water drops away as well. However, there are no immediate rivers, streams or water channels of any kind flowing away from the lake. Roughly one kilometre from Loughareema, lies a completely dry river bed. Around the corner, a rapidly flowing spring emerges gushing from the ground, as if by magic. Using a traceable dye, this powerful gushing current has been proved to be the water which was once held in Loughareema, and which has somehow spent two days travelling here through some mysterious underground network that no one has been able to follow.

Adding to this unusual spot is the odd fact that the amount of water emerging from this spring is twice the volume of what was contained within Loughareema. Where is the extra water coming from? The leading theory is that this whole landscape could be peppered with a hidden network of underwater channels, a series of tiny connected cracks within the rock, through which water can be transported between lakes and rivers in a way in which the local residents have forever been completely unaware. It's just one of the many mysteries yet to be explained about this strange feature of the Northern Irish countryside.

RIGHT: The rapid rising and falling of the water level is a key feature of Loughareema.

ISOLATED REALMS

21° 13' 29" N / 51° 7' 10" E

EMPTY QUARTER
Saudi Arabia/Oman/UAE

Salalah–Doha

Huge chains of sand dunes rising up to 1,000ft high and stretching for hundreds of miles towards a desolate, featureless horizon. Unpredictable, marshy quicksand, reported to have swallowed up passing travellers. Scorpions, snakes and even Arabian wolves, red foxes and desert lynx, all battling for survival in an environment that receives less than an inch of rain each year. Far from civilisation, in an area covering 250,000 square miles, larger than the entirety of France, lies the Rub' al Khali – the Empty Quarter.

'The broadest expanse of unexplored territory outside of Antarctica' was how the New York-based Explorers Club described the Empty Quarter in 1930. At the time, this vast desert landscape, nestled between several Gulf countries – particularly Saudi Arabia, Yemen and what is now the Sultanate of Oman and the United Arab Emirates (UAE) – was at the centre of a race to be the first to successfully navigate its formidable dunes. 'Nothing but an airship can do it,' had been the assessment of the great T.E. Lawrence (Lawrence of Arabia).

Briton Bertram Thomas aspired to prove such doubts wrong. Setting off secretly in late 1930 from Salalah, Oman (he had feared that by asking permission he might be refused and so went ahead without being officially sanctioned), he and his expedition partner Sheikh Salih bin Kalut al Rashidi al Kathiri trekked with fifteen camels and a caravan of local Bedouin nomads through Oman, suffering with intensely hot days and freezing cold nights, gradually trudging their way across the Empty Quarter. 'Under an eastern sky crayoned with crimson and gold,' Thomas later described the desert in his book *Arabia Felix*, 'in the far distance a sunlit yellow ribbon now edged the skyline.' They pressed on relentlessly through the desert until, two months after setting off, they arrived in Doha, Qatar. After a brief trek to Bahrain, to access a working telegraph, their success made front-page headlines around the world.

BAGHDAD

IRAQ

Tigris

Euphrates

Basra

KUWAIT

Isfahan

Zagros Mountains

Dasht-e Lut

IRAN

Kerman

Shiraz

Bandar-e Abbas

Persian Gulf

BAHRAIN

QATAR

Doha

Dubai

Abu Dhabi

UNITED ARAB EMIRATES

Muscat

SAUDI

Medina

RIYADH

ARABIA

Mecca

EMPTY QUARTER

(Rub' al Khali)

OMAN

Abha

Salahah

Red Sea

SANA'A

Al Hudaydah

YEMEN

Al Hudaydah

Arabian Sea

Taizz

Aden

Gulf of Aden

Socotra

N

DJIBOUTI

ETHIOPIA

Berbera

SOMALIA

Bertram Thomas' route, 1930

0   250 miles

0   250 kilometres

Following in Thomas's footsteps became an aspiration for a generation of explorers, but for most it remained only a romantic ideal. However, in 1932, another English explorer, Harry St John Philby, crossed the Quarter in the opposite direction, while renowned explorer Wilfred Thesiger famously followed in their footsteps and embarked upon his own torturous missions in the late 1940s, describing the Empty Quarter as 'the final and greatest prize of Arabian exploration' in his pivotal book *Arabian Sands*. 'Bertram Thomas proved that this desert was not impassable as was once supposed,' he wrote. 'To remain there for long would test myself to the limit. Much of it was unexplored. It was one of the very few places left where I could satisfy an urge to go where others had not been.' In crossing the desert twice between 1945 and 1949, thoroughly surveying the landscape as he and his companions passed through, Thesiger added his own name to the hallows of history, an iconic figure of Arabian exploration.

This location has long been a draw for ambitious explorers, helped immensely by the romantic tales and photographs of figures such as Lawrence in the 1920s. 'A teasing mistress, that beckons only to forbid' is how Thomas described his own relationship with the Empty Quarter. 'The Empty Quarter offered me the chance to win distinction as a traveller,' wrote Thesiger, 'but I believed that it could give me more than this, that in those empty wastes I could find the peace that comes with solitude, and, among the Bedu, comradeship in a hostile world.'

The native Bedouin, or Bedu, have been essential travelling companions for Empty Quarter explorers ever since Thomas. Their knowledge of the landscape, simply 'the Sands' as they called it, including navigable routes and the locations of usable drinking

wells, enabled these iconic figures to create history. Today, many of these nomadic communities have left the remoteness of the desert in favour of more economically productive locations around the coast of the Arabian Peninsula. The loss of such people from the Empty Quarter – and the loss of the rich cultural encyclopedic knowledge contained in the heads of their ancestors – has been to the detriment of aspiring explorers, leaving them somewhat less informed about the challenges they face than would have been the case last century.

In recent years, the Crossing the Empty Quarter expedition, organised by another Briton, Mark Evans, followed Thomas's exact footsteps in late 2015, trekking for forty-nine days from Salalah to Doha, a journey which continued to generate headlines globally. 'Our experience was a long way from that experienced by Thomas, and far less uncertain,' Evans recalls, 'but the physical landscape is as challenging as it has always been – here, nature is firmly in control; no technology can prevent or predict a sandstorm, or predict whether the water in the next well will reek of sulphur, or be drinkable. Other than the remains of long-abandoned oil exploration camps, we saw no sign of human activity outside of our party for some thirty days, and were privileged to travel through a sea of sand so enormous that not even the widest angle of lenses could truly capture the enormity, and the beauty.' Even well into the twenty-first century, it's never-ending remoteness and inhospitality ensures the Empty Quarter remains a vast and unruly patch of wilderness, arguably now emptier than it has been for generations.

BELOW: The sand dunes of the Empty Quarter can be as much as 1,000ft high.

16° 16' 57" S / 36° 22' 54" E

THE MOUNT MABU RAINFOREST
MOZAMBIQUE
Mount Mabu

It can be sobering, in the twenty-first century, to acknowledge the gaps that remain in human knowledge of the world, even if they happen to yield positive outcomes. One such example is what has been nicknamed the 'Google forest'. This remarkable area of dense vegetation, covering 30 square miles of northern Mozambique, was until very recently completely unknown to the scientific community.

That changed in 2005, when Julian Bayliss, a British biodiversity scientist, happened to be browsing Google Earth – the tech giant's virtual mapping software – looking at sites nearby to Mount Mulanje, an isolated site in southern Malawi where he had been recently working for the Mulanje Mountain Conservation Trust. Sat at his computer in north Wales, he found his attention particularly being drawn towards a number of mysterious mountains just inside the Mozambique border. Distinct among the lighter colours of the surrounding landscape, a few dark-green patches on the satellite picture significantly stood out for him. 'There was virtually nothing written about these mountains,' he explains. He didn't know it at the time, but Bayliss had discovered what would turn out to be the largest rainforest in southern Africa, a 'vast, pristine area of medium-altitude forest bursting with biodiversity', according to Kew Royal Botanical Gardens, London.

In December 2005, Bayliss and his team arrived on the ground in Mozambique, to further explore these mountains. 'I set about choosing which mountains we should visit,' he recalls. 'The initial criteria was mountains over fifteen hundred metres [5,000ft]. This is generally when things start to get interesting in terms of biodiversity and endemism. Species tend to become isolated at these altitudes and therefore possibly new to science.' The first attempt to reach the peak of Mount Mabu was unsuccessful, the team running out of water three-quarters of the way up a steep slope. In the distance, beyond the

mountain peak and onwards to the horizon, they sighted the green patch which Bayliss had spotted on his computer back in the UK. Here, following an alternate route the following day, they discovered a wild and essentially untouched landscape, quiet and peaceful except for the faint chorus of chirping from distant birds and insects. 'The first visit was tremendously exciting,' he enthuses. 'This is when we first saw and entered the forest, and confirmed what we had suspected, that it was indeed rainforest.' Exploring the tangled, lush vegetation of the interior, cool and dense under the shade of the forest canopy, yielded dramatic findings, including vast numbers of birdlife, plants and insects, many of which were entirely new to science.

In late 2008, Bayliss returned to Mount Mabu, part of an international expedition led by Kew Royal Botanic Gardens and funded by the Darwin Initiative (a UK government scheme intended to protect natural biodiversity in the developing world). Compared to the poor state of the tarnished landscape surrounding the rainforest – primarily due to the decade-long civil war that ended in 1992, leaving the region less populated now than it was fifty years ago – the site itself was assessed to be in as pristine a condition as the scientists had hoped. Limited access, as well as a lack of knowledge of its existence – the only human activity having occurred there being the occasional use as a refuge for villagers from the fighting – had helped protect this remarkable environment. The team found a diverse mix of unique species, including rare orchids, pygmy chameleons, Swynnerton's robin and other vulnerable birds, as well as a number of previously unknown snakes. A report produced in 2014 by Bayliss and colleagues, states: 'the high number of endemic species discovered on Mount Mabu and surrounding mountains suggests a long period of isolation . . . more discoveries of new species are expected.'

The Mount Mabu rainforest has also been called the Butterfly Forest, as a result of the vibrant and dramatic butterfly displays that have been witnessed there, as hundreds of colourful species congregate together around the summit. 'It is very exciting!' confirms Bayliss. 'At first you think there is nothing happening, then all of a sudden the air becomes full of many different types of butterfly.' The phenomenon lasts for less than an hour, normally starting in the late morning during the beginning of the wet season, around October and November. Several entirely new species of butterfly have been found in the forest, one of which, the *Cymothoe baylissi*, carries the name of the man who stumbled upon the rainforest in the first place, while simply browsing maps on his computer.

'It is like discovering lost worlds on a par with the earlier Victorian explorers. And there are a lot of similarities, as one can still only get to these areas on foot with a team of local porters over the course of several weeks', describes Bayliss. 'It is a rare find, that much is true. However it is not necessarily the case that we have discovered all that there is to find. I think there are still plenty of places to discover and explore.'

ABOVE: The untouched rainforest of Mount Mabu
was only discovered from Google satellite images.

17° 45' 0" N / 10° 4' 0" E

TREE OF TÉNÉRÉ

NIGER

Ténéré Desert

It can get lonely out in the desert, surrounded by vast emptiness, with nothing but shifting sand dunes for miles around. With over 4,000 hours of sunshine per year, and temperatures therefore regularly exceeding 38°C (100°F), it's none too comfortable either. Pity, then, what was dubbed 'the most famous tree in Niger', the so-called Tree of Ténéré (l'Arbre du Ténéré): an acacia tree which for over 300 years stood in the middle of a dreary Saharan wilderness, the only vegetation for 250 miles in any direction. For centuries, this single shrub acted as a key landmark for passing nomads and merchants, particularly the trans-Saharan salt traders travelling along the ancient 375-mile caravan route from the southeastern end of the Aïr mountains, to the small-town oasis of Fachi way out to the east. Drawing on deep water supplies as far as 130ft below the surface, the popular Tree of Ténéré found itself noted on countless maps and historical records of the region. It was a rare highlight for passing travellers amid the dusty, monotonous and intensely hot Saharan landscape.

The surrounding Ténéré Desert, combined with the rocky Aïr mountains, forms Africa's largest protected area – the Aïr and Ténéré Natural Reserves – a coming-together of two sharply contrasting landscapes covering a total of 30,000 square miles. It's a unique wildlife hotspot, with forty species of mammals identified in the reserve – including specialist desert carnivores such as fennec and Rüppells foxes, both of which possess comically large ears to help cool off in the desert heat, plus the critically endangered Saharan cheetah – as well as 165 species of birds and 18 species of reptiles. Furthermore, roughly one-sixth of the reserve has been specially designated as a sanctuary for the protection of addax (also known as the screwhorn antelope), with the fractured populations sporadically dotted around the Aïr mountains the last holdout for the species.

ABOVE: The remote Tree of Ténéré was an iconic desert landmark for centuries. Following its demise, a simple metal sculpture was raised to pay tribute to the fallen tree.

The Aïr and Ténéré Natural Reserves were originally listed as a UNESCO World Heritage Site in 1991, described as an 'outstanding example of geological processes, biological evolution and man's interaction with his natural environment', thanks to highly significant findings such as enormous dinosaur 'graveyards', as well as detailed archaeological records. These include vivid cave paintings of giraffes, rhino and antelopes, demonstrating how the region has been inhabited by indigenous Tuareg nomads for over 30,000 years. However, just one year later it found itself officially downgraded to 'in danger', thanks to 'political instability and civil strife' stirred up by Tuareg separatists who caused several years of civil unrest in the early 1990s in the hope of achieving their own independent, autonomous state. As the violence migrated up into the Aïr mountains, the remote region became an extremely dangerous and volatile location. While a peace agreement was eventually achieved in April 1995, the dissatisfaction among Tuareg communities clearly hasn't abated, since the past two decades has repeatedly seen bouts of violence flare up again in Niger and neighbouring Mali, adding to the unpredictability about the future of the region.

Salt caravans, passing the Tree of Ténéré, once consisted of tens of thousands of camels trekking across the desert landscape. In recent years these have been replaced by trucks, as the modern world has caught up with even this isolated part of the world. Sadly, one of these trucks was to lead to the demise of the tree in 1973, when a driver – a little inebriated, if rumours are to be believed – managed somehow to crash his vehicle into essentially the only obstacle for miles around. History doesn't record what state the truck ended up in after this incident, but the pieces of the tree were lovingly collected and subsequently placed on display at the National Museum in Niamey, the capital of Niger. In its place, where the original, ancient tree stood for centuries, a strange alien-like metal structure was erected, installed in tribute to the beloved Arbre du Ténéré.

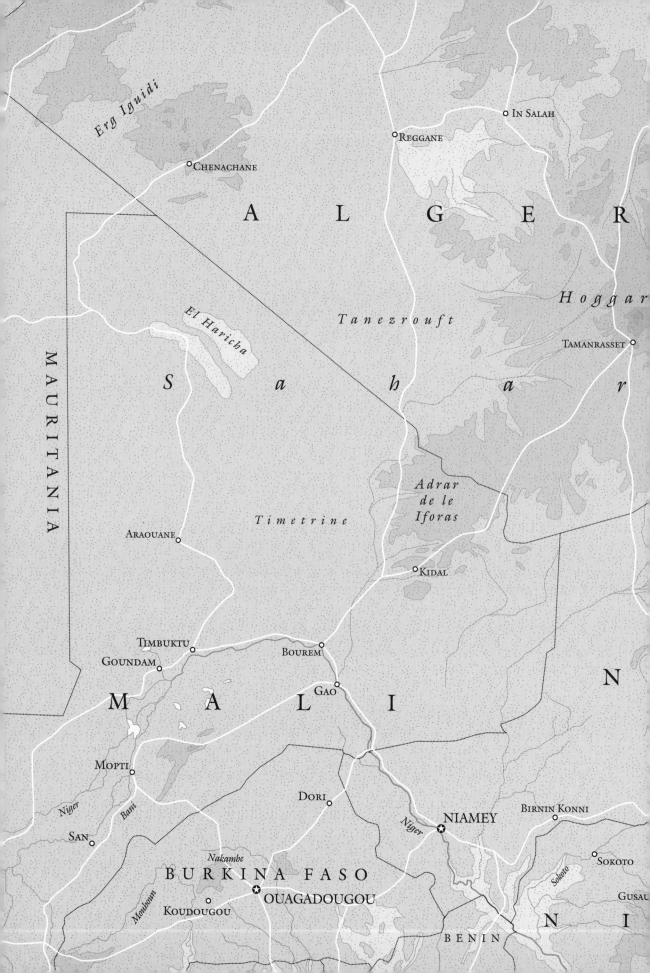

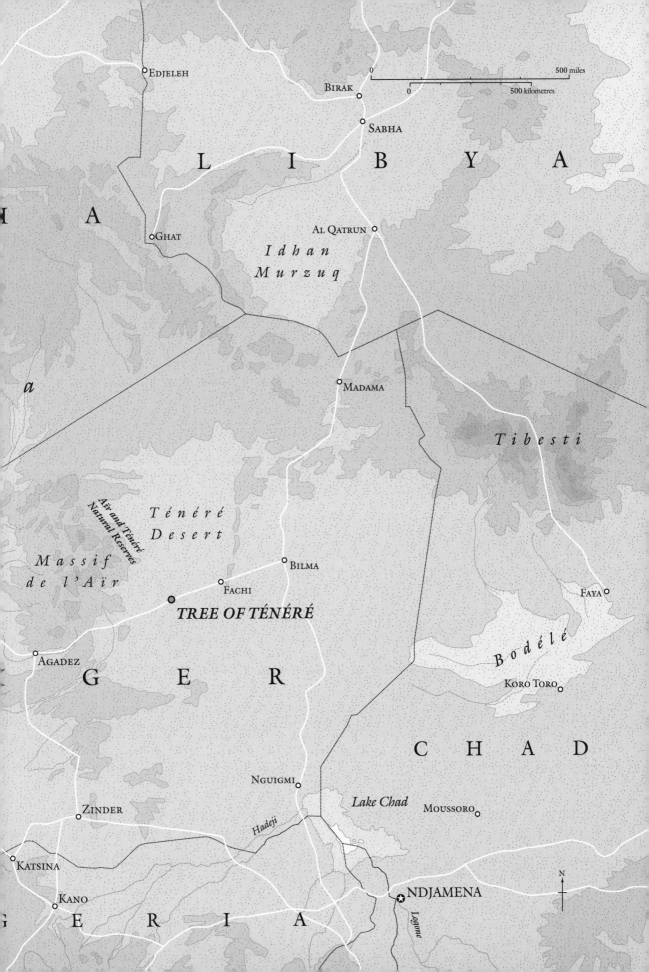

4° 15' 24" N / 52° 58' 54" W

ININI
FRENCH GUIANA
Saint-Élie

There is a part of France, far from the grandeur of the Eiffel Tower and the Champs-Élysées, where people still live a primitive existence, with almost no rule of law. Across the Atlantic Ocean, and down into the deep Amazon rainforest interior of French Guiana, this underdeveloped territory, Inini, remains technically part of modern-day France, yet is also an almost unexplored frontier of the fifth French Republic. The discovery of gold led to the region being likened by an early twentieth-century investigative French journalist to the mythical 'El Dorado'. The French first arrived on the continent in the seventeenth century, officially establishing the capital of Cayenne (La Ravardière) in 1643. The territory became a penal colony for more than 70,000 prisoners from the mid-nineteenth century for nearly a century, particularly Île du Diable – Devil's Island – a rocky outcrop ten miles offshore.

There is, however, a world of difference between the coastal capital of Cayenne and the other modern, globalised port settlements around which most of the 257,000 mainly Creole population lives, and the mysterious deep tropical jungle to the south, which covers 90 per cent of the 32,000 square miles of the territory. Much of the Inini region remains almost inaccessible, dense forest essentially disconnecting it from the outside world. It became a separately governed territory in 1930, followed by the entire French Guiana region becoming a *département d'outre-mer* (overseas department) just sixteen years later, alongside the likes of Guadeloupe, Martinique and Réunion. The Inini territory was then officially abolished in 1969 in an attempt to integrate the remote indigenous inhabitants with the rest of French Guiana, and wider French society.

Once upon a time, the big business here was gold mining. The town of Saint-Élie, former capital of Inini, was founded by prospectors in the nineteenth century. But as the

MANA

MOENGO

ALBINA
ST LAURENT

ORGANABO

IRACOUBO

SINNAMARY

Maroni

ATLANTIC

Devil's I.

OCEAN

APATOU

GARE TIGRE

SAINT-ÉLIE

KOUROU

CAYENNE

N

ROURA

*Sinnamary
Reservoir*

CACAO

Mana

Comté

GUISANBOURG

GRAND SANTI

RÉGINA

Lawa

F R E N C H

Sinnamary

G U I A N A

Approuague

CORMONTIBO

S U R I N A M

ININI

MARIPASOULA

CLÉMENT

Oyapok

MALAVATE

BIENVENEU

CAMOPI

Camopi

Litanie

Marouini

Serra Lombarda

Tumucumaque

B R A Z I L

Jari

0   50 miles

0   50 kilometres

▨ Inini, 1930–46

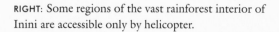

RIGHT: Some regions of the vast rainforest interior of Inini are accessible only by helicopter.

world entered a depression through the late 1920s and early 1930s, gold production went into decline. Inini particularly suffered. Saint-Élie and other towns that had once been sites of golden prosperity amid this otherwise wild terrain became derelict, with only a handful of residents. The abandoned town can now only be accessed either by helicopter, or via an epic journey involving a long narrow dirt road for miles through the jungle, followed by a boat ride, and finally a jeep or quad bike trip across rugged terrain. The whole trek can take as long as two days. In the early days of the 2000s, the town became the centre of an illegal gold mining scandal, an incident which saw the active intervention of the French Military Forces in order to prevent the situation getting out of hand.

The over-1,600 indigenous residents of the Inini territory, primarily Amerindians and Maroons, are often unrecorded by the authorities, yet are all members of the European Union. Even in January 2015, a survey of the population uncovered a

25-year-old man who had somehow slipped through the hands of the state, avoiding all previous registrations. With the breakdown of both the self-sufficiency lifestyle of past generations, and the law and order which came with a thriving gold industry, the Amerindians became left behind from the rest of France, trapped in their lawless jungle territory.

In 2015, French photographer Christophe Gin spent months battling his way back and forth across French Guiana, documenting the unique lives of the people he met. The expedition was funded by the Carmignac photojournalism award, Gin commented on Inini: 'I don't see it as a lawless territory, but rather as a region composed of unique enclaves, and shaped by the French Republic,' he said. 'This territory is one of the last areas of freedom, and has now become a collection of zones operating outside the laws of the French State.'

83° 38' 30" N / 31° 28' 28" W

KAFFEKLUBBEN ISLAND
GREENLAND
Peary Land

The world's southernmost point on land is relatively easy to locate: the static South Pole on Antarctica. In the north, however, the vast Arctic ocean makes it harder to pinpoint the equivalent spot; what has historically been known as *Ultima Thule*, the northern edge of the known world. It first gained prominence following the account of Pytheas, a Greek explorer who hailed from Massalia (modern day Marseille) around 2,300 years ago. Though his most famous work, *On the Ocean*, has since been lost, rumours of his expeditions were nevertheless passed down through word of mouth, century after century. Pytheas journeyed through western Europe, including the Mediterranean, Britain and Scandinavia, and believed he had reached *Ultima Thule*. Given he had likely made his way only to Norway or, at a stretch, Iceland, he was considerably far from being correct, but perhaps we can forgive him this error, given the limits of the knowledge of the world at the time.

In 1900, Robert Edwin Peary, an American explorer, decided he had settled the question once and for all. Trekking north up Greenland, he established, first, that the vast island didn't extend all the way to the North Pole. Furthermore, he discovered a large area to the north, a frozen and mountainous 200-mile-long coastline occasionally torn apart by fjords. He believed that one specific spot, now known as Cape Morris Jesup – 440 miles from the Pole – was the world's northern most piece of land. 'It was evident to me now that we were very near the northern extremity of the land,' he wrote in his expedition report, 'and when we came within view of the next point ahead I felt that my eyes rested at last upon the Arctic Ultima Thule.' Peary was fixated on reaching the North Pole itself, and believed he had done so in 1909, on his third attempt. While this achievement has subsequently become a contentious, controversial issue, with experts

ABOVE: The remote Peary land is the final *terra firma* before embarking upon the world's most northerly recorded land, which only emerges seasonally from beneath the Arctic ice.

re-examining his diaries and maps, and disagreeing as to whether he reached the top of the world, or only got to within 30–60 miles of it, his finding of Cape Morris Jesup (as well as Peary Land, the large, frozen region of northern Greenland which now bears his name) remains an iconic mark in Arctic exploration history.

Two decades later, in 1921, the Danish explorer Lauge Koch and his crew were navigating their way along the far Arctic northern coast of Greenland, 23 miles east of Cape Morris Jesup, when an island was sighted roughly a mile off shore. No land was known to exist this far north, with only the ice-covered Arctic Ocean believed to be found between Cape Morris Jesup and the North Pole. Koch named this new island Kaffeklubben – meaning 'Coffee Club' – Island, a tribute to an association of academic geographers back in Copenhagen. Studies in 1969 concluded that Kaffeklubben Island was definitively further north than Cape Morris Jesup by a mere half a mile, confirming this dreary island as the iconic *Ultima Thule*.

Peter Skafte, polar scientist, described Kaffeklubben Island as looking 'like a gigantic stranded whale about two-thirds of a mile long' when recalling his 1996 expedition there in the American Polar Society's journal *The Polar Times*. 'Even on these bare windswept slopes, flowers cling to the gravel,' he wrote. 'Out of curiosity I walked to the northern tip of the island to locate the world's northernmost individual flower. It was a purple saxifrage, only an inch tall, yet a conqueror here at the edge of the world.'

Is this, then, the most northerly land in the world? In 1978, a new island was spotted. Named Odaq (or Oodaaq), it was rumoured to be even further north than Kaffeklubben, yet subsequent attempts to locate it and verify claims of it being the true *Ultima Thule* were hit and miss, the island often nowhere to be seen. It now appears to be a permanent, yet frequently invisible, area of land, one of the so-called 'ghost islands' which Skafte, among others, has since spotted in this part of the world. 'Odaq Island, as well as a number of other islands in the same area, are basically low sandbars with a few rocks that only stick up about a metre above sea level,' he explains. These other islands include Top of the World Island, Turtle Island, and the imaginatively named 83-42 (its coordinates). 'These features are only visible during maximum snow and ice melt at the end of August,' he adds. 'Even a light snowstorm will render them invisible.'

Either way, as the Arctic, like the South China Sea and other large water bodies, enters a period of intense geopolitical tug-of-war, it is likely that the romantic *Ultima Thule* vision will give way to a more hard-nosed and pragmatic perspective on what exactly constitutes the world's most northern point of land. At least Kaffeklubben Island – a small, otherwise insignificant speck of land on the edge of the inhospitable Arctic – remains a true, natural northern 'edge of the world', whatever may come in the future.

37° 18' 1" S / 12° 40' 24" W

INACCESSIBLE ISLAND
South Atlantic

Tristan da Cunha

Tristan da Cunha, part of the UK Overseas Territory of St Helena, Ascension and Tristan da Cunha in the South Atlantic, is a grouping of some of the most remote islands in the entire world. It is home to only 267 residents, who make a living primarily through fishing, including exports of the local Tristan rock lobster. The nearest airport is in Cape Town, South Africa, 1,750 miles of South Atlantic ocean away, meaning trips to and from the islands come via a handful of six-day journeys aboard fishing and research vessels, which also transport all necessary fuel, food and mail.

Sometimes, a name says it all. The uninhabited Inaccessible Island, one of the islands comprising the Tristan da Cunha archipelago (the other main islands being Tristan da Cunha island itself, Gough Island and Nightingale Island), takes this isolation one step further. Though the island, the eroded remnants of a 6,000,000-year-old volcano, was supposedly first discovered by the Dutch ship *t'Nachtglas* while scouting Tristan da Cunha in January 1656, it is believed to have received its name when French sea captain Captain d'Etchevery, of the ship *Etoile du Matin*, found himself daunted by the vast plateau-like shape of the island, sticking over 1,000ft vertically up out of the sea, during a pass in 1778. (Its highest point, Cairn Peak, collects snow at the summit.) These dramatically sheer sea walls, which act as a natural defence for the island, also host spectacular waterfalls, as a network of streams empty their contents into the sea. Once an aspiring visitor has traversed the epic journey all the way to Tristan da Cunha and then onwards to Inaccessible Island, battling extreme, unpredictable weather conditions, they must then deal with the island's seemingly impenetrably steep cliffs in order to attempt a landing.

Efforts by individuals to settle permanently have had little to no success. Closest to achieving this goal were the German Stoltenhoff brothers, who attempted to colonise

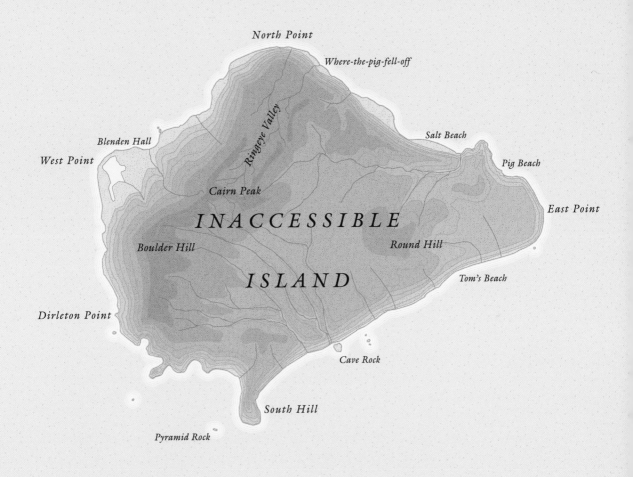

SOUTH ATLANTIC OCEAN

North Point

Where-the-pig-fell-off

Ringeye Valley

Blenden Hall

Salt Beach

West Point

Pig Beach

Cairn Peak

INACCESSIBLE

East Point

Boulder Hill

Round Hill

ISLAND

Tom's Beach

Dirleton Point

Cave Rock

South Hill

Pyramid Rock

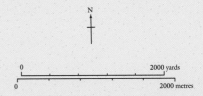

N

0		2000 yards
0		2000 metres

the island in 1871, but were forced to abandon the project after just two years when they ran desperately low on food. Half a century earlier a number of sailors found themselves forced into such a situation: their ship, the 450-ton East Indiaman *Blenden Hall,* was en route to Bombay (modern-day Mumbai, India) but drifted off course and ran aground on Inaccessible Island in July 1821, after striking rocks just offshore. Surviving on wild celery, penguin eggs, and seal, penguin and petrel meat for four months, the ship's survivors eventually built a new boat, which was able to sail to Tristan da Cunha for help. In January 1822, exactly six months after the disaster, they were finally rescued and taken to the mainland. The spot on Inaccessible Island where they landed, now itself named Blenden Hall, is a constant reminder of the island's most famous shipwreck.

The waters around Inaccessible Island were declared a nature reserve in 1997 and, in 2004, it joined with neighbouring Gough Island to form the 'Gough and Inaccessible Islands' UNESCO World Heritage Site. Thanks to the unique process of evolution which unfolded there, the flora and fauna of Inaccessible Island include at least two bird species, eight plant species and ten invertebrate species not found anywhere else in the world. They are home to the critically endangered Tristan albatross, Gough finch and Atlantic petrel, as well as the Inaccessible rail – the smallest flightless bird in the world – and many

other rare species that nest on the sheer Atlantic cliffs. The island is also home to the striking northern rockhopper penguin, with its flashy yellow crest, and is an important breeding ground for more than two million pairs of great shearwaters.

Additionally, since Inaccessible Island's natural fortifications have kept humans away for so many years, there has been significantly less human interference in its environment than across most of the world. Only recently have invasive house mice begun to cause problems, preying as they do on helpless chicks, leading to a severe decline in many populations (mice and rats having already caused havoc and extinctions on many similarly isolated islands). Some rogue pigs that were once introduced did have a good try at snuffling out many native species, but the pigs failed to establish themselves and died out before causing too much damage – good news for the island's delicate biodiversity.

ABOVE: Steep cliffs surrounding the isolated Inaccessible Island give the island its name.

65° 46' 56" N / 168° 58' 34" W

DIOMEDE ISLANDS
USA/RUSSIA

Diomede

The Bering Strait, on the fringes of the Arctic Circle in the far north of the Pacific Ocean, represents a meeting point between two vast continents. During the Cold War, it essentially served as a frontier between the world's two superpowers, their fingertips reaching out towards each other, but never quite touching (the narrowest point between the two landmasses is a mere 53 miles).

In the middle of this pivotal geographical oddity lie the Diomede Islands, bleak granite rocks emerging from the mist. They come as a pair – Big Diomede, on the Russian side of the line (Ostrov Ratmanova in Russian), and Little Diomede on the American side. At only two and a half miles apart, they are the closest connection between the full stretch of the strait. The International Date Line runs through the middle, separating the islands by a full twenty-four hours. Rather wonderfully, they are therefore sometimes known as Tomorrow Island and Yesterday Island. In winter, temperatures can dip below -18°C (below 0°F), enabling a frozen bridge to form between the islands, allowing the strait to be crossed on foot, a crucial component in the colonisation of the Americas with wildlife and humans migrating millennia ago. Here is where cultures collide. Here is also where cultures are ripped apart.

'The dreariest towns I ever beheld' was the less-than-positive assessment of John Muir, the Scottish-American naturalist known as the 'Father of the National Parks', when he visited Little Diomede in 1881. 'The tops of the islands in gloomy stormclouds,' he recalled for his book *Travels in Alaska*, 'snow to the water's edge, and blocks of rugged ice for a fringe; then the black water dashing against the ice; the grey sleety sky, the screaming water birds, the howling wind, and the blue gathering sludge.' The traditional inhabitants of the Diomedes were the indigenous Iñupiat, who lived in this frigid

DIOMEDE

ISLANDS

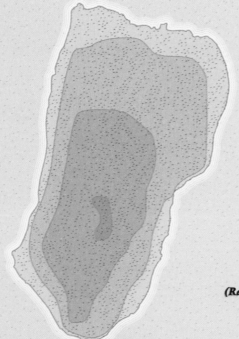

INALIK o
(Research Station)

Big Diomede

Island
(Russia)

Little Diomede

Island
(USA)

BERING   STRAIT

International Date Line

N

environment for thousands of years. Where once all of the Iñupiat were free to travel and hunt between the two islands, the twentieth century brought a harsh dose of geopolitical reality. During the Second World War, the residents of Big Diomede were forcibly removed by the Soviet Union, settled elsewhere in the country, and the island turned into a military and scientific base. When the Cold War cooled diplomatic relations between the two nations, the islands became completely disconnected, the relationship between the once-close communities entirely terminated. With the Russian Iñupiat becoming assimilated into Russian culture, forbidden ever to return to their island, and their Alaskan cousins increasingly bound by the lifestyle that came with being an official citizen of the United States of America, the Diomede culture wilted, almost ceasing to exist. The unique Ignaluk language, once prevalent across the two islands, became lost forever. The hardening of the 'ice curtain' in recent years has only served to further divide these

LEFT: Geopolitics collides with natural forces when two continents meet at the Diomede Islands.

communities. Big Diomede exists as a stark, barren, steep-cliffed landscape, while the few remaining inhabitants of Little Diomede maintain a simple existence devoid of normal American luxuries, such as alcohol. As a result, the islands themselves, now increasingly abandoned, are arguably more wild than they have been in generations.

Due to the unique geographical positioning of the Diomede Islands, they have provided the backdrop to some extraordinary moments in history, especially in the dying days of the Cold War. In 1987, American swimmer Lynne Cox braved temperatures of 3°C (38°F) to swim between the two islands, a symbolic act in response to any travel between the pair having previously been completely banned. Both US President Ronald Reagan and his Soviet counterpart Mikhail Gorbachev congratulated Cox on her remarkable feat, and the way she managed to bring these two continents just that slightly bit closer together.

69° 34' 46" N / 139° 4' 34" W

HERSCHEL ISLAND

Canada

Yukon

Far up in northern Canada, roughly a mile off the shore of the Yukon region, and covering an area of just 45 square miles, is Herschel Island. 'To an island the Centre of which bears about 15 miles distant I have given the distinguished name of Herschel,' records the journal of Sir John Franklin, dated 15 July 1826, on his second expedition into the Canadian Arctic. His book of the expedition, *Narrative of a Second Expedition to the Shores of the Polar Sea, in the Years 1825, 1826, and 1827*, claims it to have been 'much frequented by the natives at this season of the year, as it abounds with deer, and its surrounding waters afford plenty of fish'. Indeed, the island was a popular hunting spot for the local Inuvialuit Inuit population, who called it Qikiqtaruk (simply meaning 'island').

Two decades after discovering Herschel, Franklin headed back to the region. He and his ships, HMS *Erebus* and HMS *Terror*, were hunting for the fabled Northwest Passage between the Atlantic and Pacific Oceans. They never returned. Not until the 2010s were the ships eventually discovered, having been trapped by ice, crushed, and eventually lost to the sea. However, the man who did eventually successfully navigate the passage, the legendary Norwegian explorer Roald Amundsen, did so by making use of Herschel Island in 1905.

Thanks primarily to the whaling industry, this was once a thriving part of the country, a speck of economic activity otherwise surrounded by icy desolation. The small town of Herschel was the regional hub for sailors, whalers and indigenous Inuvialuit people heading out to sea in search of the riches which barrels of whale oil – harvested from the carcasses of successfully captured beluga and bowhead whales – could provide. (To a lesser extent, the town also provided income for fur traders and gold prospectors.) An estimated 1,200 inhabitants lived in Herschel at the end of the nineteenth century.

Having made it through the Northwest Passage, Amundsen needed to send a message to his sponsors, informing them of his success. Leaving most of his crew amid the whalers and fur traders on the island, he sledged across the frozen sea ice to the mainland, before following the Firth and Porcupine rivers to Fort Yukon, Alaska. Unfortunately, the settlement didn't have the telegraph system he required to notify the world of his achievement, meaning he had to continue his journey south to Eagle, travelling over 700 miles across the Yukon. Having sent his message, and waiting an incredibly slow two months for a reply, he turned round and began the long journey back. Even more treacherous than his route down, the return journey north saw him plough through frigid Arctic terrain as he made his way back to his ship the *Gjøa*. Amundsen's epic journey illustrates just how remote is the part of the world where Herschel Island lies. Following a successful return journey, Amundsen would go on, six years later, to become the first person to reach the South Pole.

Amundsen's journey to Eagle and back was replicated for the first time in 2016 by the explorer Tim Oakley and his team, crossing the same rivers and gorges as Amundsen had done 111 years earlier. 'You're very exposed, there's just nothing there now, it is just a vast country,' revealed Oakley to *Geographical* magazine. 'The first river has got a lot of canyons and gorges, and class-four rapids in it. So, to travel with dog sledges on that,

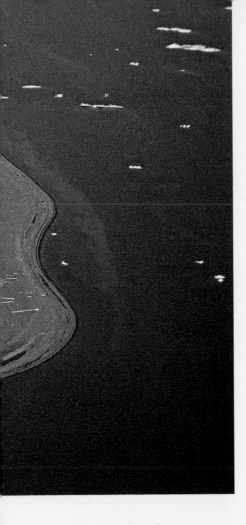

once you're into those gorges, you are committed. There is no other way around the situation.' Oakley and his team spent six days trekking along the river, slowly progressing at around fifteen miles a day. Occasionally they would encounter rapids where the ice had broken, meaning they had to drag the sledges up steep slopes of highly polished 'glare ice', all the while doing everything in their power to stay warm amid temperatures capable of dropping as low as -50°C (-58°F), a painfully authentic recreation of the reality which Amundsen would have experienced over a century earlier. 'Of course, when you come out of the water with your boots in those temperatures it immediately freezes, then you have to use an axe to get your boots off, which can take half an hour. It was pretty difficult.'

In 1907, the global whale oil market collapsed, and with it the local whale hunting industry. Consequently, by the late 1980s there were no residents left on Herschel Island whatsoever. Now the remote town of Herschel, several miles inside the Arctic Circle, sits empty, a vessel of memories to past prosperity. Cabins sit boarded up, the trails that once ferried produce south for trade now quiet and empty, in many cases reclaimed by the wilderness. With its extreme northern location placing it right on the frontline of climate change, even the Inuvialuit stay away, their traditional subsistence hunting threatened by melting ice and severe coastal erosion. It's a far cry from the 'hotspot' discovered by Franklin nearly two centuries ago.

NATURE'S WILDERNESS

INDIAN OCEAN

QALANSIYAH ○   *Ra's Kadarma*   *Ra's Hulaf*
    ○ QAYSOH   *Qadama Beach*   HULAF ○
                                        HADIBOH
                              MORI ○ ○
      GHUBBAH ○   ○   ○ QADUB
                    QASHIO

                                            ○ JO'OH
Ra's Shu'ab   *Jabal Haggier*

S O C O T R A   *Ra's Momi*

(Yemen)

                    N a w q i d
Ra's Qatanan   *Aomak Beach*
                        STERO
                        ○

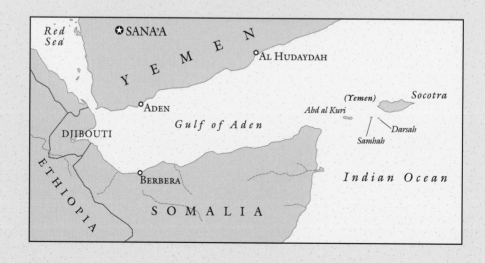

🝰 *Darsah*

Red   ✪ SANA'A
Sea
                        ○ AL HUDAYDAH

            Y   E   M   E   N

                                                    (Yemen)
                                                              Socotra
          ○ ADEN   *Gulf of Aden*   *Abd al Kuri*
DJIBOUTI   →*Darsah*
                                              Samhah
ETHIOPIA
            ○ BERBERA
                                        Indian Ocean
        S   O   M   A   L   I   A

12° 27' 48" N / 53° 49' 25" E

SOCOTRA

Yemen

Gulf of Aden

Dragon's blood. It sounds like an ingredient for a medieval potion, but it is in fact a deep-red resin that for centuries has been prescribed in many traditional communities as a cure for all manner of medical and cosmetic issues. Skin lesions? Dragon's blood. Eye disease? Dragon's blood. Heartburn? Take dragon's blood. The resin has historically been used for everything from dyeing clothes and varnishing wood, to adding decorations in traditional pottery. Historically, it has also been recognised as the blood of the biblical figures Cain and Abel, hence the name still in use in much of the Arab world, *dam al akhawayn*, meaning 'blood of the two brothers'.

Although it is often used as a catch-all name for the resin collected from any of the Dracaena plants, a distinctive type of shrub, dragon's blood primarily refers specifically to the rich liquid contained within the dark berries of *Dracaena cinnabari* – the 'dragon's blood tree'. This strange-looking plant is found in only one place in the world: the other-worldly island of Socotra.

Located 200 miles off the Yemeni mainland, and perched off the end of the troubled Horn of Africa, the hot and arid Socotra – one 82-mile-long main island, with five smaller accomplices within the archipelago – has become renowned for its bizarre appearance, a consequence of its historical isolation. Although not as physically remote as many other islands, the continental (as opposed to volcanic) bedrock of the island means it has spent far longer cut off from the outside world. Inclusive of the dragon's blood tree, the island is home to at least 307 completely endemic plants (37 per cent of its total 825 plant species), including the peculiarly tall and bare cucumber tree, and the desert rose, with its bright pink flowers. Socotra's fauna is just as diverse and unique as its flora, with 90 per cent of its 34 types of reptiles, and 95 per cent of its 96 land snail species, not found anywhere else in the world. Its particular location also means it serves as an important breeding and resting point for hundreds of both local and migrating birds, while the surrounding turquoise waters are home to a recorded 730 species of fish, 300 species of crab, lobster and shrimp, and hundreds of types of reef-building corals. It's no surprise that Socotra is often described as the most alien-like place on Earth.

Yet this delicate haven of biodiversity is at risk. The widespread but fragmented dragon's blood tree is listed as 'vulnerable' by the International Union for Conservation of Nature and Natural Resources, threatened by hungry goats that have been introduced to the island, a gradually increasing drought, and occasional deforestation as locals explore alternative industries, such as the keeping of bees. Furthermore, the illustrious history of dragon's blood may be small in relative terms, but any potential rise in demand could place the few trees on Socotra under intense pressure, as harvesters, their eyes fixed on the profits to be made by exporting this product around the world, extract the resin in ever larger quantities. Numbers of dragon's blood trees are declining; while they were once found all over the island, now they are located only in sporadic patches. Socotra's unique ecosystem may already have experienced its golden years, as the outside world turns up knocking at its door.

In 2011, it was widely reported that Somali pirates were using Socotra's strategic location as an offshore base for refuelling and launching their crafts in pursuit of profitable cargo ships. Villainous criminality and dubious politics aside, it's a nod to the ancient history of the island, which has been a favoured hotspot for piracy on the high seas for over a millennium – a real-life Treasure Island. 'A multitude of corsairs [pirates] frequent the Island,' recalled the famous thirteenth-century traveller Marco Polo, 'they come there and encamp and put up their plunder to sale; and this they do to good profit.' For centuries, Socotra earned a sinister reputation as a brutish den for pirates and their nefarious deeds. Hence, while the modern pirates may have been banished from the island for now, the prime location of Socotra, at the end of the Gulf of Aden, and its unique environment that has fascinated and attracted people for millennia, continues to play by its own rules.

RIGHT: Socotra Island is famed for the iconic
'dragon's blood tree', but is also home to a variety of
unusual flora.

33° 41' 49" S / 20° 40' 39" E

CAPE FLORAL REGION
SOUTH AFRICA
Cape Town

'All that I had pictured to myself of the riches of the Cape in botany, was far surpassed by what I saw in this day's walk,' wrote English explorer and naturalist William Burchell in his 1822 travelogue *Travels in the Interior of Southern Africa, Volume 1*. 'At every step a different plant appeared; and it is not an exaggerated description, if it should be compared to a botanic garden, neglected and left to grow to a state of nature.'

For centuries, botanists had yearned to be able to properly categorise the world's flora. Numerous nineteenth-century botanists attempted to devise logical ways to organise the physical space of the floral world. However, it was the seminal work of British botanist Ronald Good with his book *The Geography of the Flowering Plants*, first published in 1947, which could be flagged as the breakthrough moment. Good theorised that the world could be divided into six 'floral kingdoms': vast, continent-crossing swathes of the planet with similar environmental conditions and therefore capable of sustaining similar plant species. Five of these six are the temperate land of North America and Eurasia known as Holarctic; the Paleotropical region of sub-Saharan Africa and India; the Neotropical region of Central and South America; the Australian region; and the Antarctic region.

Standing out precisely because of its relatively diminutive size, the Cape Floral Region – found in the southwest of South Africa – covers a mere 35,000 square miles, slightly smaller than Portugal. This tiny area is so uniquely wild and biologically diverse that it is counted as an entire floral kingdom all by itself. While the Cape Floral Region represents less than 0.5 per cent of the area of Africa, it is nevertheless home to nearly 20 per cent of the continent's plant species, and as much as 69 per cent of its 9,000 plants are completely unique to the region (the Table Mountain National Park alone is home to more plant species than the entire British Isles). This is why UNESCO describes the Cape Floral Region as 'one of the world's "hottest hotspots"'.

One key plant here is fynbos, a tough and highly flammable shrub that has specially evolved to live in the unique environment of the Cape's infertile soils; it is found nowhere else in the world. An incredible 8,500 different varieties of fynbos shrubs inhabit the Cape, and are therefore the key reason for the region's immense diversity. The region is prone to wildfires thanks to how easily fynbos catches alight, and these fires are believed to be key to the rapid recycling of nutrients and the dispersion of seeds which has created such a diverse number of localised species. Planned 'prescribed burning' now takes place to enable fynbos to rejuvenate without posing an out-of-control threat.

While the region is a highly researched part of the world for the scientific community, it is also a popular spot for so-called 'citizen scientists', who undertake small-scale conservation and research. Arguably the most proactive are the Outramps. This hardy group of senior citizens travel back and forth across the Cape Floral Region in their 'Buchu Bus', monitoring the region's threatened plant life, and discovering several new species in the process.

ABOVE: South Africa's Cape Floral Region has some of the world's highest density of unique plant species.

CAPE

Karoo

○ CARNARVON

○ BRITSTOWN

○ DE AAR

HANOVER ○

MIDDELBURG ○

○ Orange

GRAAFF-REINET ○

CRADOCK ○

○ BEAUFORT WEST

SOMERSET EAST ○

○ RIETBRON

EASTERN CAPE

Groot

Swartberg
Mountains

UNIONDALE ○

Baviaanskloof
Reserve

DESPATCH ○

○ OUDTSHOORN

○ KNYSNA

○ GEORGE

Cape Seal

HUMANSDORP ○

PORT ELIZABETH ○

○ MOSSEL BAY

Cape
St Francis

INDIAN OCEAN

World Heritage Sites — Cape Floral Region

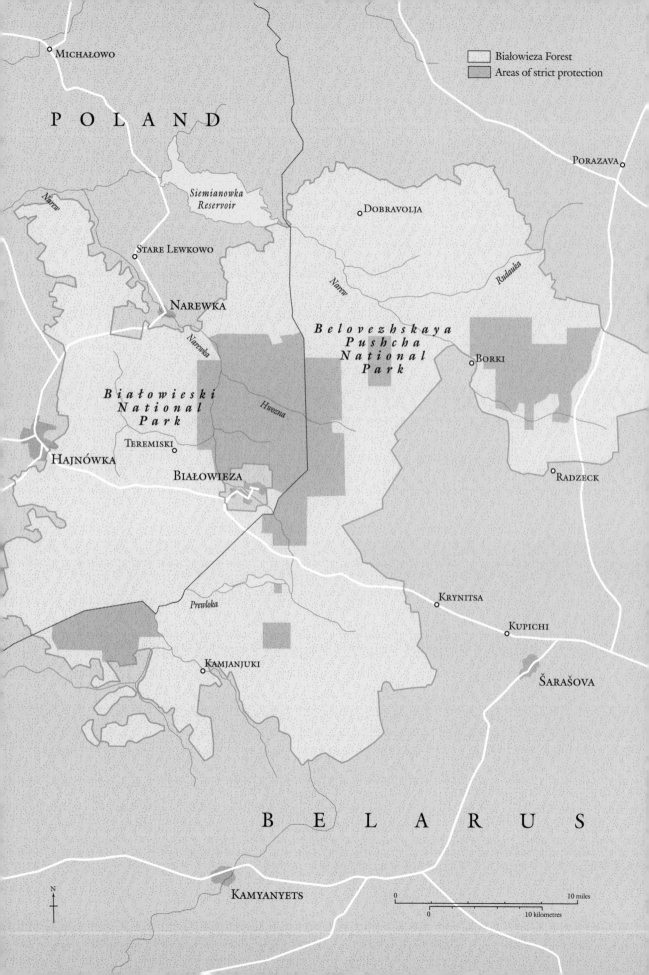

BIAŁOWIEZA FOREST

POLAND/BELARUS

Białowieza

Satellite images of Europe at night depict a gigantic network of bright lights, long streams connecting blotches of dense, urban hubs. Once upon a time, however, it was home to a great primeval forest, full of enormous, thick woodland, populated by all manner of large animals. Aurochs, a kind of primitive cattle, would have grazed in diverse meadows, alongside wild boar, deer and tarpan (a kind of wild horse). Sadly, centuries of extreme human dominance on the European continent has seen this great forest cut back further and further, to the point that it's hard to envisage a natural European landscape underneath layer upon layer of asphalt and concrete.

There is one corner of the continent where the remnants of this great forest have held out, even into the twenty-first century. The ancient Białowieza Forest, a mystical landscape of dead wood, fallen trees and clusters of mushrooms straddling the border between Poland and Belarus, is a 580 square miles primeval haven of natural wilderness which has held out against the incursions of the modern world. Home to otters, lynx, and even wolf packs, it has also played host to the recovery of the great European bison (zubr) in recent years, with an estimated 900 individuals believed to now live in the forest. The entire woodland is an exciting emporium of temperate untamed land, with a varied landscape including wild meadows, diverse river corridors, wetlands and vast tree canopies. With species such as 300–400-year-old oak and ash trees reaching to a height of 130ft – plus gigantic fir trees pushing 160ft – it's a romantic vision of a long-forgotten Europe, the final glimpses of an environment that has otherwise been lost across the whole continent.

Because of a particular cocktail of historical events, this unique area of land resisted the conversion to agricultural land to which most neighbouring environments were subjected. For over four centuries, as Europe morphed and modernised between 1385 and

1795, the Białowieza Forest was granted explicit protection as hunting grounds for royalty. Here, successive Polish kings would take their entourages out for multi-day hunts in search of bison, brown bears and moose. The forest was out of bounds for most ordinary folk, but locals would be recruited to maintain the health of the natural ecosystem, through occasional forest-clearing and coppicing (when a tree is cut down and encouraged to regrow, often considerably lengthening its lifespan). They could sometimes use the land for hay-making, bee-keeping and the removal of timber – when given permission by the crown – while the wildlife within was occasionally used for supplying salted venison for military campaigns across the Polish–Lithuanian Commonwealth.

In 1795, the forest changed hands and for 120 years found itself under Russian rule. This initially meant it lost its royal protection, but in 1802 the new Russian owners deemed it worthy of similar conservation practices, with tsars granting hunting permits to royalty and prestigious guests. Białowieza Forest took on a significance far beyond the Russian border, as an important anchor point for national folklore across this part of Europe. In 1820, German forester Julius von Brinken described this *Urwald* (German for a primeval forest) as 'a thing of glory and terror'. In Germany, Białowieza was the embodiment of a nostalgic search for home, the so-called *Heimat*, and 'liberating' the forest into German hands was a significant military and cultural achievement in both 1915 and 1941. Around this time, the forest served as hiding places for Jewish families fleeing occupation, a story made famous by the 1993 book *Defiance* by Nechama Tec, and subsequent 2008 Hollywood adaptation starring Daniel Craig. Post-war, the forest was spliced in two by the new Polish–Soviet border – later to became a border with Belarus following the country's declaration of independence in 1991 – and officially designated a UNESCO World Heritage Site in 1979.

Predictably, however, even this final sanctuary of Europe's wilderness remains under threat. In 2016, the Polish government ruled for a tripling of deforestation in their share of the forest, roughly 16 per cent of which is protected as a national park, in response to an infestation of spruce bark beetle discovered in the forest, which they claimed was getting out of control. However, critics of the government's plans argued this is just part of the natural regeneration of the forest, something that has been part of its ongoing evolution over thousands of years. The fate of hundreds of bison and other wildlife could depend on the outcome of this decision.

RIGHT: Some of Europe's last remaining natural forest can be found in the Poland–Belarus border region.

0° 5' 17" N / 38° 11' 24" E

MERU NATIONAL PARK

Kenya

Meru

Many people will be familiar with the *Born Free* story – the Joy Adamson novel that became a 1966 film starring Virginia McKenna and Bill Travers, which went on to Oscar success thanks to John Barry's iconic musical score. The setting for this emotive story of the young lion cub Elsa being reintroduced to the wild is Meru National Park, 200 miles north of Kenya's capital, Nairobi. In recent years, a fascinating experiment has been under way in this region of northern Kenya, a revolutionary attempt to restore the natural African environment, in a place that was decimated by punishing conflicts and utter abandonment. What has emerged is a remarkable tribute to the immense restorative power of nature.

Helped by *Born Free*, Meru during the 1970s and 80s was a hotspot for Kenya's booming tourism industry. However, as the years passed (and with the retirement and passing of leading conservationists such as Peter Jenkins and George Adamson, who had both been hugely influential on the ecological health of the park), it began to fall into disrepair, with much of the infrastructure falling apart. Local farmers, many of whom were suffering from severe drought and the effects of regional conflicts, spied an opportunity to grab some land for their cattle, while poachers and desperate villagers realised that the relatively unguarded park animals in Meru had become valuable prize trophies. Without the protection they desperately needed, the native animal populations of Meru were annihilated, up to 90 per cent of its animal populations disappearing during the 1990s. Elephants, which had numbered around 3,000 in the 1970s, had fallen to fewer than 300 by 1991, while rhinos were wiped out altogether. The land became almost lawless, overrun with armed bandits, and visitor numbers plummeted as a result.

Looking at the decrepit mess which the once-great Meru National Park had become, a collaboration of organisations, led by the International Fund for Animal Welfare (IFAW),

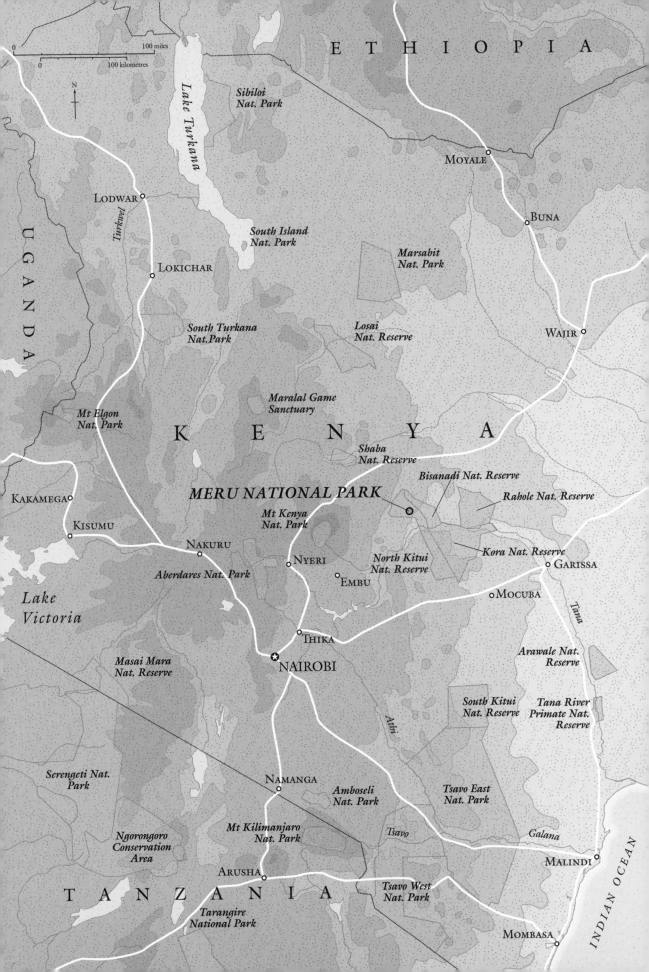

the Kenya Wildlife Service (KWS) and the French Development Agency (AFD), approached the Kenyan government with a proposition: if they could be given control of the land at Meru, they felt they could bring the natural environment back to life and rekindle the park from the scarred ashes which had been left behind. The government agreed, and the project began. Barriers were constructed around the park, and new teams of security personnel assigned to patrol the borders. Animals were transported into the park from wherever they could be found, courtesy of the highly experienced KWS 'Capture Unit'. More than 1,300 different wildlife species were packed into Meru, an area of 335 square miles. Finally, they stepped back, and simply waited to see what would happen. No specific areas were set aside or cordoned off for any particular species; it was left to the natural order to take charge, and recreate an unpredictable – in theory 'authentic' African landscape – in this wild environment.

The results were startling. Far from the managed game parks observed across Africa, where the native fauna often inhabit the same spaces as cattle and other livestock, Meru

became evidence of what could happen when nature was simply left alone, and allowed to 're-wild' itself. Flying over the park reveals a sharp juxtaposition between the deep red earth across most of the surrounding, semi-arid landscape, and the thick, lush greenery that explodes from within the park boundaries. Giraffes, impala, elephants and endangered Grévy's zebra – distinguishable from the common zebra by their comical, Mickey Mouse-like ears – all thrive in the park. An in-depth survey conducted by KWS and the Born Free Foundation revealed the park's carnivores holding firm, with healthy populations of lions, as well as spotted hyenas and leopards. At a time when species such as wild lions are experiencing a sharp decline across most of Africa (likely now fewer than 20,000 across the whole continent, down from 100,000 in the 1980s, 450,000 in the 1940s, and as many as one million in 1900) thanks to human-lion conflict – so-called 'revenge killings' – as well as the increasing trade in lion body parts for 'traditional' medicines, it's an encouraging sign that the Meru experiment has been a success, and a potential way forward.

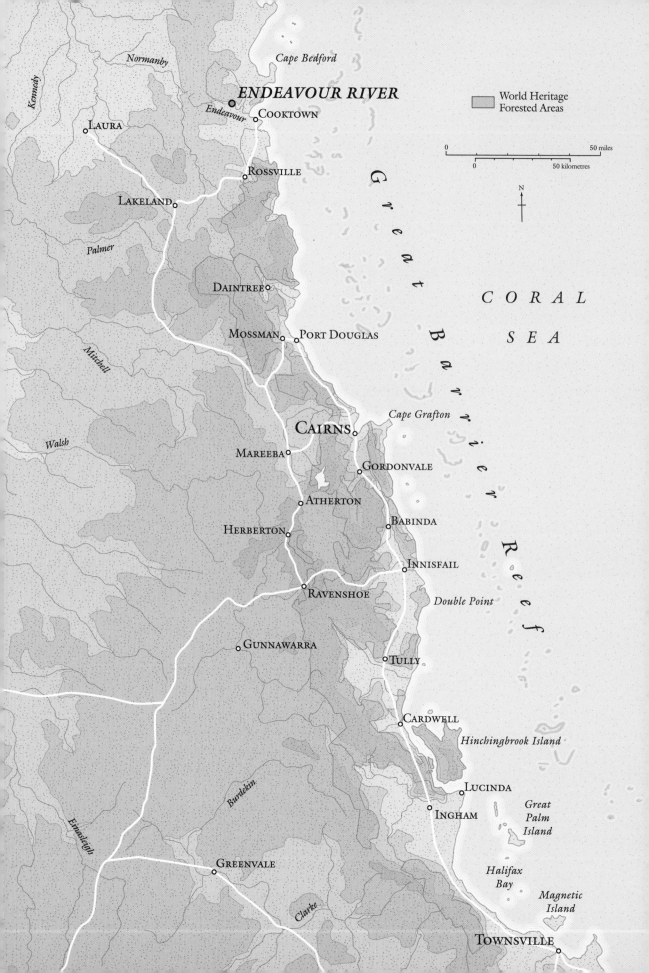

Normanby

Kennedy

Cape Bedford

ENDEAVOUR RIVER

Endeavour COOKTOWN

LAURA

ROSSVILLE

LAKELAND

Palmer

DAINTREE

Mitchell

MOSSMAN PORT DOUGLAS

Walsh

Cape Grafton

CAIRNS

MAREEBA

GORDONVALE

ATHERTON

BABINDA

HERBERTON

INNISFAIL

RAVENSHOE

Double Point

GUNNAWARRA

TULLY

CARDWELL

Hinchingbrook Island

Burdekin

LUCINDA

Einasleigh

INGHAM

Great Palm Island

GREENVALE

Halifax Bay

Clarke

Magnetic Island

TOWNSVILLE

World Heritage Forested Areas

Great Barrier Reef

C O R A L
S E A

50 miles

0

0   50 kilometres

N

ENDEAVOUR RIVER

AUSTRALIA

Cooktown, Queensland

Captain James Cook faced a problem. Having sailed from England, round Cape Horn on the tip of South America, and down to New Zealand, he had settled in Botany Bay, and secured for himself a leading spot in Australia's history forever. However, soon after he and his crew began the navigational route northwards on the long journey home in mid-1770, they encountered significant difficulties. His ship the *Endeavour* found itself navigating an extremely narrow channel between submerged reefs – what we now know as part of the world-famous Great Barrier Reef. 'Here began all our troubles,' Cook wrote in his journal. Striking a hidden reef, the *Endeavour* became impaled with coral, and was in desperate need of repair. 'This was an alarming and, I may say, terrible circumstance, and threatened immediate destruction to us,' he continued.

Heading for the shore, they settled in a narrow channel at the mouth of a nearby river with plentiful fish, turtles and fresh water. In tribute to the occasion, Cook named the waterway the Endeavour River. They would spend seven weeks in this same spot, as the repairs required by the ship were gradually undertaken. This delay gave Cook the opportunity to do something he hadn't managed in the now far more famous Botany Bay; to actually leave the ship for an extended period of time. He and the crew slept on the land, explored the surrounding landscape, and interacted with the continent's unique wildlife. 'It was of a light mouse colour and the full size of a Grey Hound, and shaped in every respect like one, with a long tail, which it carried like a Grey Hound,' wrote Cook, of his first encounter with a kangaroo. 'I should have taken it for a wild dog but for its walking or running, in which it jump'd like a Hare or Deer.' He also engaged amicably with the local Guugu Yimithirr, his first proper encounter with Australia's indigenous Aborigines, while at the Endeavour River (which the native people had always called Waalumbaal Birri).

His notes record that their voices were 'soft and Tunable', and that, while both men and women lived naked ('without any manner of Cloathing whatever'), the women decorated their bodies with shell necklaces and bracelets, and many of the men wore a bone 'about 3 or 4 Inches long and a finger's thick' through the bridge of their nose.

In the twenty-first century, the Endeavour River remains the name of the channel that flows through the settlement of Cooktown before exiting into the Coral Sea. It sits at the northern tip of the world-famous Wet Tropics of Queensland, a UNESCO World Heritage Site of 3,500 square miles and stretching 280 miles along northern Queensland, down to Townsville. A 'stunningly beautiful area' according to UNESCO, it comprises probably the oldest tropical rainforest on Earth, and 'presents an unparalleled record of the ecological and evolutionary processes that shaped the flora and fauna of Australia, containing the relicts of the great Gondwanan forest that covered Australia and part of Antarctica 50 to 100 million years ago'.

Home to everything from ringtail possums to tree kangaroos to the spotted-tailed quoll (Australia's largest carnivorous marsupial), it holds 35 per cent of Australia's mammals in just 0.2 per cent of its land area. With over 4,000 plant species – such as the Gympie-Gympie stinging tree, one of the most venomous plants in the world – 40 per cent of Australia's bird species, including the notoriously aggressive southern cassowary, and a remarkable 60 per cent of its butterfly species, it is undoubtedly a biodiversity hotspot within what is otherwise well known as a relatively dry and arid continent.

This diversity extends to many of Australia's infamously dangerous animals, from highly poisonous snakes such as the red-bellied black snake, the eastern small-eyed snake, and the tree-climbing rough-scaled snake, to the terrifying saltwater crocodile (the fabled 'saltie'). As with much of tropical northern Australia, the Endeavour River sees its fair share of crocodile-related incidents: stories of people – often unsuspecting tourists – disappearing from the river's banks appear in local and national news every few years.

38° 45' 17" S / 177° 9' 33" E

TE UREWERA
NEW ZEALAND

Wairoa

What if wild places, like people, had fundamental rights? What if a natural landscape could become a 'legal entity', enabling it to possess the same constitutional liberties as a human being? How different would such an obviously unrealistic utopian world be? Except, this isn't a work of fiction. In 2014, the New Zealand government passed the revolutionary Te Urewera Act, which, among other things, granted the forest of Te Urewera, in the country's North Island, 'all the rights, powers, duties, and liabilities of a legal person'.

Te Urewera is a misty and remote 820 square miles area of land filled with thick forest, formed millions of years ago when the muddy, silty and sandy bedrock beneath was forced up and out of the sea, and then carved through for millennia by the north-flowing rivers of Whakatane, Waimana and Tauranga. It became a national park in 1954, the highlights of which are Lake Waikaremoana (the 'sea of rippling water'), an area of 20 square miles and the smaller Lake Waikareiti, both located in the south of the park, and both hotspots for tourism in the region, drawing hikers and boaters to this natural wilderness. Yet, some sections of the park are so inaccessible that even these hardy visitors don't venture in. They therefore remain remote ecosystems with healthy populations of native wildlife, including iconic and endangered national birds such as kiwi, kokako, and kaka. The park's unique forests host over 650 types of native plants, including everything from short, moss-covered beech trees, to ancient endemic podocarp giants such as rimu and kahikatea, species which can grow to a dizzying 165–195ft tall.

For the indigenous Māori people, the Ngāi Tūhoe (known as the 'children of the mist'), Te Urewera is far more than a mere natural playground for tourists. According to their traditional legendary ancestry, the Tūhoe are the descendants of the marriage

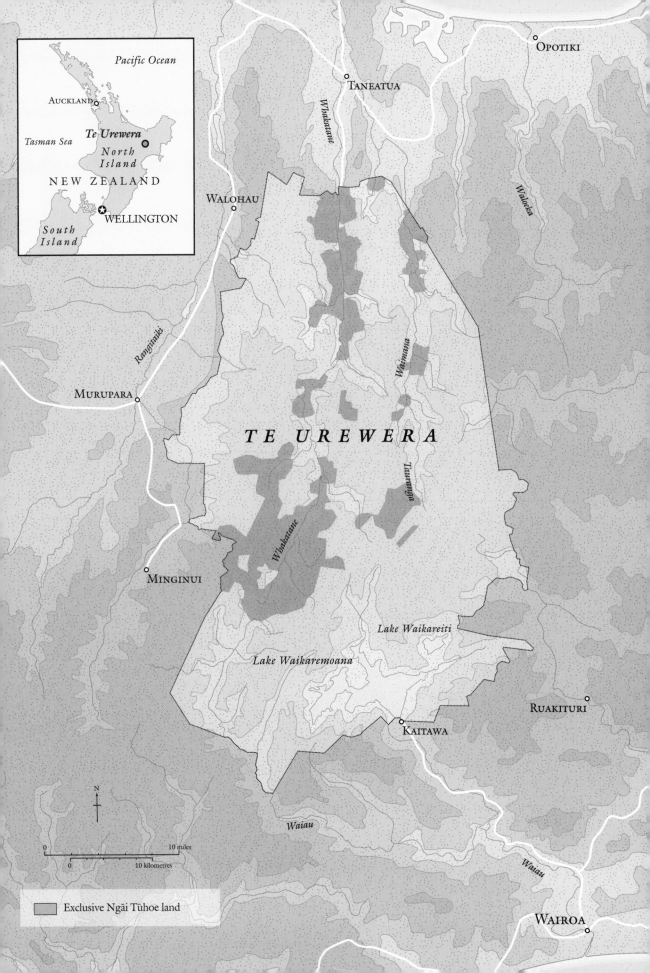

Pacific Ocean

AUCKLAND

Te Urewera

Tasman Sea

North
Island

NEW ZEALAND

WELLINGTON

South
Island

OPOTIKI

TANEATUA

Whakatane

Waiohia

WALOHAU

Waimana

Ranginaki

MURUPARA

TE UREWERA

Tauranga

Whakatane

MINGINUI

Lake Waikareiti

Lake Waikaremoana

RUAKITURI

KAITAWA

N

Waiau

0   10 miles

0   10 kilometres

Waiau

WAIROA

Exclusive Ngāi Tūhoe land

between Te Maunga (the mountain) and Hine-Pokohu-Rangi (the mist maiden), making this dramatic and mystical landscape completely intertwined with their identity. 'In their worldview, "I am the river and the river is me", explained Chris Finlayson, New Zealand's attorney general, at the conclusion of the court case which led to the Te Urewera Act. 'Their geographic region is part and parcel of who they are.'

When large numbers of Europeans arrived in New Zealand in the middle of the nineteenth century, the Tūhoe fiercely resisted, waging war against the British Crown during the 1860s and '70s in a military campaign masterminded by the charismatic leader Te Kooti. The Crown responded with force, and ultimately succeeded in banishing the Tūhoe from Te Urewera entirely, causing severe starvation and death among much of the community. As a result, the Te Urewera Act also contains apologies, and commitments to aid reconciliation between the Crown and the Tūhoe. It notes, 'Te Urewera is their . . . place of origin and return, their homeland' which 'expresses and gives meaning to Tūhoe culture, language, customs, and identity'.

The Te Urewera Act saw the Crown give up any formal ownership to the land, including its status as a national park (which was never granted with the permission of its traditional residents, the Tūhoe). Instead, it now falls under the administration of a new Tūhoe board, who 'establish and preserve in perpetuity a legal identity and protected status for Te Urewera for its intrinsic worth, its distinctive natural and cultural values, the integrity of those values, and for its national importance'.

It's a potentially revolutionary precedent. Combined with New Zealand's third-longest river, Whanganui, in the south of the North Island, also designated a legal identity (the first such classification for any river in the world), this radical new way of perceiving the natural world opens the door to legal action potentially being filed on behalf of sacred and/or environmentally or culturally significant land all over the world. The example set by the Te Urewera Act could one day enable people to stand up in court and argue on behalf of their clients: the world's wild places, with all the same legal rights as you or I.

RIGHT: Te Urewera has a deep spiritual significance to the indigenous Māori people, the Ngāi Tūhoe.

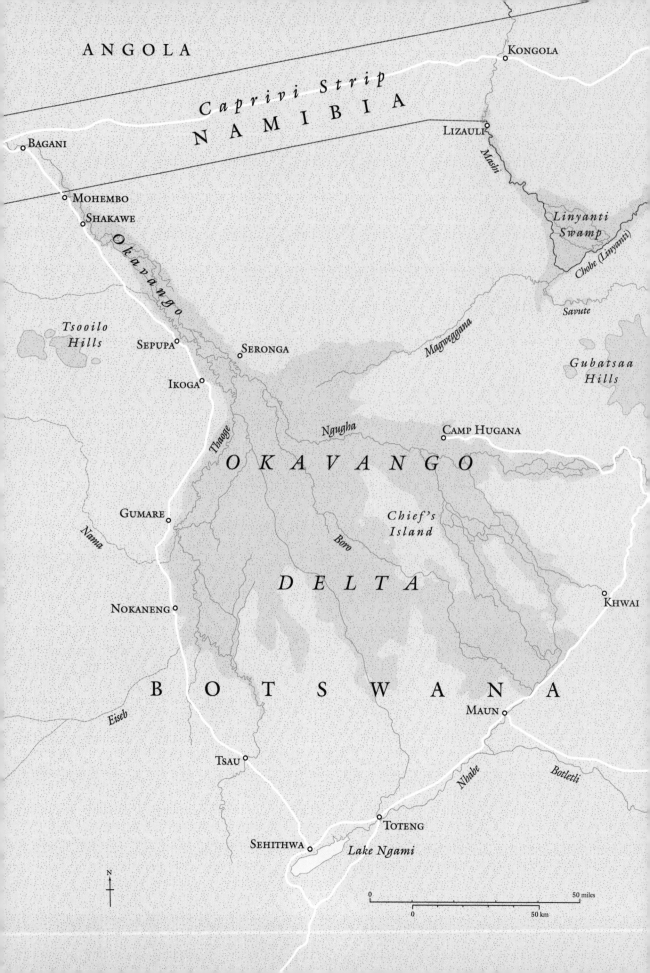

ANGOLA

Caprivi Strip

NAMIBIA

KONGOLA

LIZAULI

Mashi

BAGANI

Linyanti Swamp

MOHEMBO

SHAKAWE

Chobe (Linyanti)

O k a v a n g o

Savute

Tsooilo Hills

SEPUPA

SERONGA

Magweggana

Gubatsaa Hills

IKOGA

Thaoge

Ngugha

CAMP HUGANA

O K A V A N G O

GUMARE

Chief's Island

Nama

Boro

D E L T A

NOKANENG

KHWAI

B O T S W A N A

Eiseb

MAUN

Botletli

TSAU

Nhabe

TOTENG

SEHITHWA

Lake Ngami

N

0   50 miles

0   50 km

19° 13' 44" S / 23° 2' 56" E

OKAVANGO
Botswana/Angola
Okavango Delta

In southern Africa flows an enormous river, a great torrent of water gushing across the dry African savannah. Such a river would be expected to continue to grow in strength, as tributaries and smaller rivers reach out like tentacles and help drain the surrounding valley system into a single, dominant channel, before emptying its contents into the sea. But this river essentially does the opposite; it eventually fans out across the arid land of the Kalahari Desert, creating a vast lush oasis, before vanishing into thin air. The river is the Okavango, and the remarkable place it creates is the Okavango Delta, the 'jewel of the Kalahari Desert'.

Northern Botswana is a region whose landscape is almost entirely dominated by the presence (or absence) of water – from the distinctive fan-shape of the Okavango Delta, immediately recognisable from brief glances at satellite images of the region, to the central dry plains of the infamously inhospitable Kalahari. To fully understand the Okavango Delta, it is necessary to look to its wider catchment (the area of land which catches fallen rainwater and drains it into a single river) roughly 1,000 miles to the north: a high-rainfall zone in southern Angola. Seasonal rain falls on the Angolan Highlands of Vila Nova, on the Bié Plateau, every October, and over the next six months the fallen rain gradually flows into small channels that form the Cubango and Cuito rivers, all of which feed into the Okavango river itself. This transports the water across the Namibia panhandle, before eventually crossing the border into northern Botswana. This lengthy trip means the delta receives the highest amount of water at the driest time of year, roughly six months after the highest period of rainfall. Between February and May, when this remarkable journey ends, the Okavango Delta blooms into life. It literally doubles in size, as the water from the Okavango River floods the landscape and slowly flows through

the wetlands. It creates the perfect natural haven for the red lechwe, water-dwelling antelopes that live in large numbers among the delta's over 150,000 islands, and the 24 species of globally threatened birds, as well as wild elephants, cheetah, lions, buffalo ... even rhino and many more iconic African species that spread out across its land.

In the continent's driest place at the driest time of year – even in the middle of winter, the sun burns down hot and bright – it is remarkable that such a resource exists. As much as 98 per cent of the water that makes it to the delta ends up either simply evaporating straight back into the atmosphere or becomes absorbed by a diverse assortment of scrubby plants. The thin Boteti River transports away to the southeast the fraction that remains.

The main river channel carries only around 60 per cent of the water that ultimately reaches the delta, while the remaining two-fifths comes from a series of rivers about which significantly less is known. This is primarily thanks to decades of civil unrest in Angola. Half a million people were killed by the 27-year conflict, a time when vast swathes of the rural country became completely out of bounds. The Angolan Highlands were for a long time the heartland of the rebel movement Unita, making them far too dangerous for anyone to consider venturing into, while limited road access made this a

LEFT: The Okavango Delta is fuelled by enormous quantities of water that eventually evaporate in the hot African sun.

very difficult prospect anyway. Even today, years after a peace treaty was finally signed in 2002, millions of landmines still litter the landscape, the densest collection of such weapons still to be found in Africa. Such a deterrent to human explorers means the region is home to a pristine wilderness, almost completely untouched.

The Okavango Wilderness Project, a *National Geographic*-supported venture, has made it their mission to venture deep into these unknown parts of southern Angola, to understand the land which ultimately gives birth to the majestic Okavango Delta. This includes sending teams of explorers, scientists and local Ba'Yei people, who know the secrets to living in this environment, on a journey of hundreds of miles in traditional dugout canoes called mokoros. They travel up through the unexplored river system, passing the vast quantities of impenetrable vegetation and huge leeches, perpetually populated by aggressive hippos and enormous Nile crocodiles (the Cuito River having possibly the highest density of crocodiles in the world). 'That's the reality of this place, you're not in control of anything around you,' said project leader Steve Boyes, discussing the Okavango at a *National Geographic* event. 'You have to surrender yourself to probability, surrender yourself to the wilderness.'

1° 6' 2" S / 75° 48' 25" W

YASUNÍ NATIONAL PARK

ECUADOR

Yuturi

More than a quarter of Ecuador's population lives below the poverty line. Yet the country has great potential wealth in crude oil, billion of barrels, making oil the country's biggest export. Three particular designated oilfields – Ishpingo, Tambococha and Tiputini, known collectively as the ITT block – together contain 850 million barrels, roughly 20 per cent of the country's total oil. Such a trove could potentially sell for over $10 billion, providing funds to be invested in renewable energy and community development projects, and help lift the country out of poverty. Beside the consequential impacts of climate change (850 million barrels is equivalent to more than 400 million tons of atmospheric carbon emissions) and unreliable oil prices, there is one further problem blocking this source: the ITT block happens to sit beneath the 3,800 square mile area of the Yasuní rainforest, one of the most biodiverse in the world.

The Yasuní, 155 miles east of the capital Quito, is treasured among conservationists. It has the highest density of amphibians, birds, mammals and plants in the entire Amazon, and is home to iconic jungle wildlife such as jaguars, tapirs and capybaras. A single hectare of the Yasuní contains more native tree species – many of which reach over 100ft high, creating a dizzyingly tall canopy – than the entire USA and Canada combined. Its destruction in search of oil would be a severe blow to a world already witnessing the loss of rainforest worldwide, not to mention the havoc it would cause for the indigenous Waorani people, who rely on a healthy rainforest for their survival. Former President Rafael Correa knew this, and he knew how mining here would look to the outside world. Ecuador is home to the philosophy of *sumak kawsay*, or 'good living', which insists upon an environmentally and culturally sensitive, sustainable approach to development and lifestyle. 'We . . . hereby decide to build a new form of public

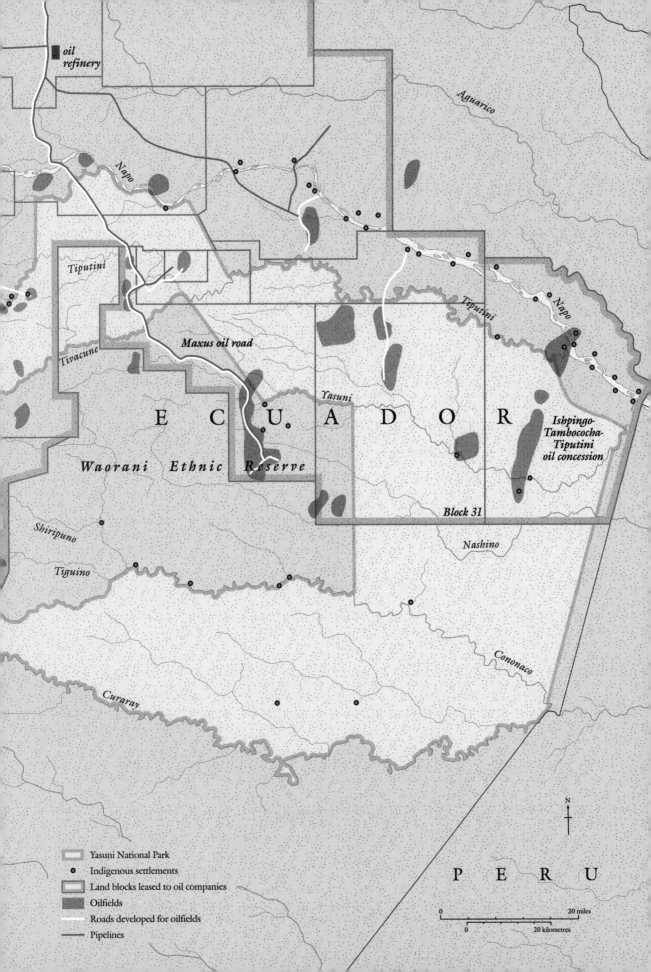

oil
refinery

Aguarico

Napo

Tiputini

Napo

Tiputini

Maxus oil road

Tivacune

Yasuni

E   C   U   A   D   O   R

*Ishpingo-
Tambococha-
Tiputini
oil concession*

Waorani   Ethnic   Reserve

Block 31

Shiripuno

Nashino

Tiguino

Cononaco

Curaray

N

P   E   R   U

☐ Yasuni National Park

● Indigenous settlements

☐ Land blocks leased to oil companies

■ Oilfields

— Roads developed for oilfields

— Pipelines

0   20 miles

0   20 kilometres

coexistence, in diversity and in harmony with nature, to achieve the good way of living,' reads a recently added paragraph to the Ecuadorian constitution. Trashing the Yasuní in search of oil would not be particularly compatible with such an ideology.

Instead, Correa came up with an idea, one that would keep the oil under the ground. 'We are arranged to make this immense sacrifice,' he announced to the international community at the 2007 UN General Assembly, 'but demanding co-responsibility from the international community and a minimum compensation for the environmental goods that we generate and from which all the planet benefits.' The plan was simple. Correa asked for wealthier nations of the world to pay $3.6 billion to the Yasuní–ITT Trust Fund, which would partially compensate the country for the revenues it would have received from drilling, pumping out and selling the oil. This would enable the Yasuní to be protected from being disturbed by tree-cutters and lumber trucks crashing through the pristine jungle. 'For the first time an oil producer country, Ecuador, where a third of the resources of the State depends on the exploitation of the above-mentioned resources, resigns this income for the wellbeing of the whole humanity and invites the world to join efforts

through a fair compensation, in order that together we lay the foundations for a more human and fair civilisation,' he declared, to a standing ovation. Contributions began to be pledged, led enthusiastically by Germany, with additional support from other European countries such as France and Italy.

However, the funds did not flow as easily and in such quantities as many had hoped. After six years, only $200m had been pledged to the fund, and a mere $13m delivered, a fraction of the desired amount. In August 2013, a resigned Correa announced the plan to have been a failure, and acknowledged that the country would be moving forward with its plans to drill the Yasuní. 'I have signed the executive decree for the liquidation of the Yasuní–ITT trust fund and through it, end the initiative,' he told an Ecuadorian television audience. In late 2016, the government announced that drilling had officially begun in the ITT, and continues to insist it can be done without significant environmental damage. Time will tell, but the fate of the Yasuní rainforest, whatever it may be, looks certain to be far more high profile, thanks to Correa's innovative scheme.

SELECTED BIBLIOGRAPHY

I am immensely grateful to the hundreds of books, academic journals and news articles that enabled me to produce this book. Organisations such as UNESCO, the CIA World Factbook, NASA, UNEP, UNDP, the NOAA, the IUCN, WWF, the Ramsar Sites Information Service, the Guinness World Records, Lonely Planet, Bradt, and the Encyclopædia Britannica, plus news media such as the BBC, Reuters, CNN, and the *Guardian*, were regularly an invaluable help. Here is a select bibliography of key texts I would like to give credit to:

- Aldersey-Williams, Hugh. *Tide: The Science and Lore of the Greatest Force on Earth*, Viking/Penguin Random House UK, London, 2016

- Berry, Steve. *Straight Up: Himalayan Tales of the Unexpected*, Vertebrate Graphics Limited, Gloucestershire, 2012

- Bramwell, David; Caujapé-Castells, Juli. *The Biology of Island Floras*, Cambridge University Press, Cambridge & New York, 2011

- Brown, Gary; Mies, Bruno. *Vegetation Ecology of Socotra*, Springer Science & Business Media, Dordrecht, Heidelberg, New York & London, 2012

- Bryan, T. Scott; Tucker-Bryan, Betty. *The Explorer's Guide to Death Valley National Park*, Third Edition, University Press of Colorado, Boulder, 2015

- Bryson, Bill. *A Walk in the Woods*, Random House, London, 1998

- Wharton, William James Lloyd. *Captain Cook's Journal during his First Voyage round the World, made in H.M. Bark Endeavour, 1768–71*, Elliot Stock, London, 1893

- Dekok, David. *Fire Underground: The Ongoing Tragedy of the Centralia Mine Fire*, Rowman & Littlefield, Guilford, 2009

- Dobraszczyk, Paul; López Galviz, Carlos; Garrett, Bradley L. *Global Undergrounds: Exploring Cities Within*, Reaktion Books, London, 2016

- Elenius, Lars; Allard, Christina; Sandström, Camilla. *Indigenous Rights in Modern Landscapes: Nordic Conservation Regimes in Global Context*, Routledge, London & New York, 2016

- Galla, Amareswar. *World Heritage: Benefits Beyond Borders*, Cambridge University Press, Paris & Cambridge, 2012

- Grundy-Warr, Carl. *Eurasia: World Boundaries, Volume 3*, Routledge, London & New York, 2002

- Howell, Paul; Lock, Michael; Cobb, Stephen. *The Jonglei Canal: Impact and Opportunity*, Cambridge University Press, Cambridge, New York & Melbourne, 1988

- Huggett, Richard J. *Fundamentals of Biogeography*, Psychology Press, London & New York, 2004

- Hund, Andrew Jon. *Antarctica and the Arctic Circle: A Geographic Encyclopedia of the Earth's Polar Regions*, ABC-CLIO, California, 2014

- Humboldt, Alexander von. *Personal Narrative of Travels to the Equinoctial Regions of America, During the Year 1799-1804 — Volume 2*, Bell & Daldy, London, 1871

- Jalais, Annu. *Forest of Tigers: People, Politics and Environment in the Sundarbans*, Routledge, Abingdon & New Delhi, 2010

- Kim, Kwi-Gon. *The Demilitarized Zone (DMZ) of Korea: Protection, Conservation and Restoration of a Unique Ecosystem*, Springer Science & Business Media, London, 2013

- Kronenberg, Jakub; Bergier, Tomasz. *Challenges of Sustainable Development in Poland*, Fundacja Sendzimira, Krakow, 2010

- Manning, John. *Field Guide to Fynbos*, Struik, Cape Town, 2007

- Martin, Pamela L. *Oil in the Soil: The Politics of Paying to Preserve the Amazon*, Rowman & Littlefield Publishers, Maryland & Plymouth, 2011

- Montgomery, Sy. *The Man-Eating Tigers of Sundarbans*, Houghton Mifflin Harcourt, New York, 2001

- Muñoz, Á. G.; Díaz L., J. E. The Catatumbo Lightnings: A Review, *XIV International Conference on Atmospheric Electricity*, Rio de Janeiro, August 2011

- Nuttall, Mark. *Encyclopedia of the Arctic*, Routledge, London & New York, 2005

- Oliver, James A. *The Bering Strait Crossing: A 21st Century Frontier Between East and West*, Information Architects, 2006

- Pelton, Robert Young. *The Adventurist: My Life in Dangerous Places*, Crown/Archetype, New York, 2001

- Polo, Marco. Edited by Wright, Thomas. *The Travels of Marco Polo: The Venetian*, Henry G. Bohn, London, 1854

- Quinn, Joyce A.; Woodward, Susan L. *Earth's Landscape: An Encyclopedia of the World's Geographic Features*, ABC-CLIO, California, 2015

- Rivera, Sheila. *The California Gold Rush*, ABDO, Minnesota, 2010

- Rogers, Stanley. *Crusoes and Castaways: True Stories of Survival and Solitude*, Dover Publications, New York, 2011

- Rudolph, Peter. *Handbook of Crystal Growth: Bulk Crystal Growth*, Second edition, Elsevier, Amsterdam, Oxford & Massachusetts, 2015

- Schmalz, Mathew N.; Gottschalk, Peter. *Engaging South Asian Religions: Boundaries, Appropriations, and Resistances*, SUNY Press, New York, 2011

- Smith, Jim; Beresford, Nicholas A. *Chernobyl: Catastrophe and Consequences*, Springer Science & Business Media, Berlin, Heidelberg & New York, 2006

- Smith, Robert B.; Siegel, Lee J. *Windows into the Earth: The Geologic Story of Yellowstone and Grand Teton National Parks*, Oxford University Press, New York, 2000

- Thesiger, Wilfred. *Arabian Sands*, Penguin UK, London, 2007

- West, Barbara A. *Encyclopedia of the Peoples of Asia and Oceania*, Infobase Publishing, New York, 2010

ACKNOWLEDGEMENTS

Firstly, I'm extremely grateful to Lucy Warburton and Aurum Press for the opportunity to pursue this project. Lucy's patient encouragement and astute feedback kept me firmly on track, and I owe her the utmost thanks. A number of talented individuals also made valuable contributions: Ashley Western's fantastic designs and Martin Brown's cartography are captivating and elevate the quality of the book to new heights; Ru Merritt did a brilliant job sourcing all our photography; while Ian Allen provided insightful and diligent copy-editing skills.

I must thank Paul Wilson from the British Geological Survey, Dr Julian Bayliss, Terry Carmichael from the Wet Tropics Management Authority, Dr Peter Skafte from the Arctic Thule Project, Philip and Charlie Mason from Elsa's Kopje, and Mark Evans from Outward Bound Oman, for generously sharing their in-depth knowledge. Of everyone who kindly suggested stories for inclusion, I must particularly thank Dr Alasdair Pinkerton from Royal Holloway, University of London.

For the opportunities I've enjoyed at *Geographical* magazine – as well as granting permission to undertake this project – I am grateful to Graeme Gourlay, as well as the rest of the team at Syon Publishing. Equally, many thanks to the iconic Royal Geographical Society (with the Institute of British Geographers) for providing the inspiration and quiet space necessary for writing, and especially Shane Winser for her positive words of encouragement.

Enormous thanks to the wonderful Rhiannon Smith for all her help, and to my friends generally for their enduring support, particularly those who assisted with research and translations. Finally, thanks to my entire intrepid family: to Grandma, for always being a twinkling ray of happiness; to Charlotte, for inspiring me with her own adventures; and lastly, to Mum and Dad, for opening my mind to the world, and always telling me to do whatever made me happiest.

PICTURE CREDITS

Alamy (eye35.pix / Alamy Stock Photo) 18–19, (Westend61 GmbH / Alamy Stock Photo) 34–35, (LatitudeStock / Alamy Stock Photo) 47, (Aurora Photos / Alamy Stock Photo) 52, 173 (Gallo Images / Alamy Stock Photo) 61, (Jong Kook Lim / Alamy Stock Photo) 89, (Zoonar GmbH / Alamy Stock Photo) 99, (RooM the Agency / Alamy Stock Photo) 121, (Xinhua / Alamy Stock Photo) 124, (Radharc Images / Alamy Stock Photo) 132 top, (imageBROKER / Alamy Stock Photo) 132 bottom, (Hemis / Alamy Stock Photo) 138–9, 150–1 (robertharding / Alamy Stock Photo) 145 left, (Arterra Picture Library / Alamy Stock Photo) 145 right, (Chris Howarth/South Atlantic / Alamy Stock Photo) 158–9, (LOETSCHER CHLAUS / Alamy Stock Photo) 166–7, (epa european pressphoto agency b.v. / Alamy Stock Photo) 175, (Lars S. Madsen / Alamy Stock Photo) 181, (mauritius images GmbH / Alamy Stock Photo) 184–5, (Andrew Watson / Alamy Stock Photo) 188–9, (age fotostock / Alamy Stock Photo) 193; AP Images 87, 68–9, 103; Getty (Hoberman Collection / Contributor) 15, (Thierry Orban / Contributor) 23, (Mario Tama / Staff) 27, (Smith Collection/Gado / Contributor) 37, (Majority World / Contributor) 43, (Jonathan Mitchell) 56–7, (Keystone–France / Contributor) 64–5, (Stephen Alvarez) 72, (Barcroft / Contributor) 77, (AFP / Stringer) 81, (DON EMMERT / Staff) 106–7, (Nicolas Fauqué / Contributor) 112–3, (ED JONES / Staff) 117, (VCG / Contributor) 127, (Jean–Erick PASQUIER / Contributor) 162–3, (Wolfgang Kaehler / Contributor) 196–7, (Tim Laman) 200–1; Mr Minton, 154–5; Nature (Hugh Pearson) 143; TopFoto (Photoshot / TopFoto) 31; USFWS (Jonsson, Kayt / USFWS) 94–5.

Brimming with creative inspiration, how-to projects and useful information to enrich your everyday life, Quarto Knows is a favourite destination for those pursuing their interests and passions. Visit our site and dig deeper with our books into your area of interest: Quarto Creates, Quarto Cooks, Quarto Homes, Quarto Lives, Quarto Drives, Quarto Explores, Quarto Gifts, or Quarto Kids.

First published in 2017 by Aurum Press
an imprint of The Quarto Group
The Old Brewery
7 Blundell Street
London N7 9BH
United Kingdom
www.QuartoKnows.com

Map illustrations by Martin Brown

A catalogue record for this book is available from the British Library.

ISBN 978 1 78131 677 1
Ebook ISBN 978 1 78131 724 2
10 9 8 7 6 5 4 3 2 1
2021 2020 2019 2018 2017

Designed by Ashley Western
Printed in China